THE
DIVINE
KISS

Life's Secret Rapture

(Al Pei Adonai – Death By The Mouth of God)

Chaim Bentorah

True Potential

REACH THE WORLD

The Divine Kiss

Life's Secret Rapture

Cover and Interior Page design by True Potential, Inc.

ISBN: (Paperback): 9781960024633

ISBN: (e-book): 9781960024640

LCCN:

True Potential

True Potential, Inc.

PO Box 904, Travelers Rest, SC 29690

www.truepotentialmedia.com

Produced and Printed in the United States of America.

DEDICATED MY GRANDMOTHER

Who told me when I was a small child that God created every green leaf for a purpose. Its mission on earth is to provide life giving oxygen, and then when it comes time to die, after fulfilling its life's calling, God gives each leaf a kiss and turns it into something beautiful.

CONTENTS

INTRODUCTION

I grew up in an evangelical church that taught the Second Coming could happen at any time. Of course, we were pre-tribulationists who believed that the Second Coming of Jesus would begin with the rapture of the church, followed by a seven-year tribulation period, ending with Jesus returning to Earth with all the saints on a white horse to single-handedly fight the Battle of Armageddon. There, He would conquer the Antichrist and all evil, establishing a thousand-year reign on Earth. All those who died in Christ would be resurrected and given a brand-new physical body.

Ah, but the really lucky ones are the Christians who will be alive when these events are initiated with the rapture of the church. All my life, I would hear preachers and Christian teachers wax lyrical about the Divine Hope of being taken alive to heaven—not having to die but being caught up from this planet by Jesus. Our physical bodies would be instantly transformed, and we would be taken to enjoy the marriage supper of the Lamb, while those who remain on Earth would suffer the unspeakable terrors and horrors of the worst tribulation humankind has ever known.

I would hear preachers clap their hands, shout "Yahoo!" and "Yippee!" and rejoice when speaking of this Divine Hope—this glorious occasion awaiting those fortunate enough to be alive when the rapture occurs. They would emphasize that we would never have to face the horrors of death. Unfortunately, many of these preachers and teachers have since "gone on to glory," as we say, without fulfilling their dream of being raptured. Or so we would assume. Was their dream of passing from this Earth without tasting death unfulfilled? I happen to believe that my beloved preachers and teachers experienced something just as wonderful as the rapture when their lives ended. They didn't miss out on anything. Yes, I believe the Scriptures teach that they never truly tasted death. Their bodies may have ceased to function, but they were too preoccupied with the *Divine Kiss* to even notice.

After many years of studying the Scriptures in Greek, Hebrew, and Aramaic, teaching Hebrew and Old Testament in Bible college, and studying Jewish history, culture, and ancient Jewish literature such as the Talmud, the Midrash, and the Targum, I have given careful consideration to this rapture business. I have decided that if the rapture occurs during my lifetime, I would choose to remain behind. I would rather tell the Lord, "I appreciate the opportunity to escape from this Great Tribulation and to bring my existence on Earth to such a glorious end through the rapture. That is quite a blessing, especially after having lived a relatively easy life of never knowing hunger because of my faith, persecution for my belief in Jesus Christ, torture for no other reason than simply loving Jesus, or experiencing martyrdom for loving the Word of God and seeking to bring others to a faith in a God who loves them—as many of our Christian brothers and sisters have experienced both today and in the past. But, you know, God, why should I escape the blessings of suffering for my faith? If it's all the same to You, I would like to stick it out in that tribulation period and see how many others I can bring into a faith in You. All I ask is that, instead of a rapture, I receive the *Divine Kiss* when that final moment comes."

When I taught in Bible college, I would share these thoughts with my classes, and many of my students would be aghast at the idea of passing up the rapture. "I would have to be a good old-fashioned fruitcake to even consider such an idea," they would say. Yet, I discovered a little secret through my studies of the Scriptures in the Biblical languages—a secret experienced by Aaron, Moses, and many of our Biblical heroes. Our Jewish brothers and sisters call it the *Divine Kiss*. I am persuaded that the *Divine Kiss* is every bit as glorious and wonderful as the rapture of the church, so much so that I call it the Secret Rapture.

After Moses had removed Aaron's garments and put them on his son Eleazar, Aaron died there on top of the mountain. Then Moses and Eleazar came down from the mountain. When the whole congregation saw that Aaron had died, the entire house of Israel mourned for him thirty days. (Numbers 20:28-2)

Now therefore, I pray thee, if I have found grace in thy sight, shew me now thy way, that I may know thee, that I may find grace in thy sight: and consider that this nation is thy people. And he said, I will make all my goodness pass before thee, and I will proclaim the name of the LORD before thee; and will be gracious to whom I will be gracious, and will shew mercy on whom I will shew mercy. (Exodus 33:13,19)

The following quote is taken from *Corrie ten Boom, The Hiding Place: The Triumphant True Story of Corrie Ten Boom*:

"Father sat down on the edge of the narrow bed. 'Corrie,' he began gently, 'when you and I go to Amsterdam—when do I give you your tickets?' I sniffed a few times, considered this. 'Why, just before we get on the train.'

'Exactly. And our wise Father in heaven knows when we're going to need things too. Don't run out ahead of Him, Corrie. When the time comes that some of us will have to die, you will look into your heart and find the strength you need—just in time.'"

As a child, Corrie ten Boom asked her father what it was like to die. Her father basically told her that when the time comes, God will give her everything she needs. Those words gave her great comfort when she was in a concentration camp facing possible death in a gas chamber. It is why countless believers have faced martyrdom with peace and joy. In their final moments, God gave them exactly what they needed to face their passing from this earth. Jewish teachers call it *The Divine Kiss*—to face death without fear or agony. God rewards the believer who has fulfilled their mission in life with a *Divine Kiss*, making their passing from this world into something beautiful. It is His way of saying: *"Well done, thou good and faithful servant."* (Matthew 25:21)

In *John 21*, Jesus explains something to Peter about the way he would die. In verse 19, we learn, *"This spake he, signifying by what death he should glorify God."*

In the Aramaic, the word for "glorify" is *shavach*, which means to rise up or to praise. What is interesting about this verse in the Aramaic is that the word *bina* is rendered as "by what." This is actually a combination of a preposition and pronoun. *Bina* is built on the root word *ina*, which has a wide range of usages in the Aramaic but carries the idea of a specific time. It was used by first-century people to describe the moment of death. This likely stems from a cultural practice where they would test if a person was dead by yelling in their ear; if there was no reaction, the person was deemed deceased.

Be that as it may, *ina* was an expression for the moment of death. Thus, what Jesus was likely telling Peter was not the specific type of death he would face, but rather that he would glorify, uplift, or praise God at the moment of death.

Peter had recently denied that he even knew Jesus to save his own life. He was grieved when Jesus asked him a third time if he loved Him. Peter faced the reality that he had put his own fleshly desires above the Savior, whom he thought he deeply loved. Yet, Jesus reassured him that there would be another time in the future when he would again face the choice of denying Jesus or proclaiming Him. This time, however, Peter would not only proclaim Him but do so joyfully, even going to his death praising the Lord. What was to change? I believe that at the moment of his death, God would do for Peter what He has done, continues to do, and will always do for believers who face their final moments—He gives them what they need to transition from this life to the next with joy and peace.

What do you need to face your final moments? What can God give you to take away any fear of death? What would cause you to echo the Apostle Paul's words: *"For me to live is Christ, to die is gain"* (Philippians 1:21)? What was it that Paul felt he had to gain, as expressed in Philippians 1:21? Was he looking for pearly gates, streets of gold, a mansion, or a heavenly home? Remember that in 2 Corinthians 12:1, Paul was caught up into Paradise. He knew what lay ahead for him after he died. Was Paul that mercenary, that materially minded? I personally doubt that very much. I believe he was on the same level as Aaron, Moses, and other believers who truly loved God with all their heart, soul, and might.

David said in Psalm 18:1, *"I love you, Lord."* The word for "love" is *racham*. However, *racham* is a word used in an imperfect inflection, indicating an uncompleted action. This should be rendered as, *"I will love you, Lord."* David understood that his love was, at best, *ahav*—the ultimate love possible in the flesh. But he also knew that one day, when his spirit was released from the flesh, he would know the true *racham* love for God.

What Paul was seeking was something he deeply longed for—the same longing that Peter and David shared. He longed to know *racham* love. There is a major distinction between *racham* love and *ahav* or *chav* love (the Aramaic cognate of *ahav*). *Chav* or *ahav* love represents the ultimate love possible in the physical realm. It is something you feel—you cannot touch it, smell it, hear it, or see it. True, the smell of your grandmother's freshly baked bread may remind you of her love. Seeing her lovingly smile at you or hearing her say, *"I love you,"* might evoke the feeling of *ahav*. But you don't literally, physically taste, see, hear, or touch her love.

Two people who share intimacy often say they are "making love." They interpret the chemical and hormonal responses of the flesh as love, but that is only a physical response. True love is ultimately spiritual. We can only know its full depths in the spiritual realm. In the physical realm, love is tangible only through manifestations, like the aroma of freshly baked bread prepared by loving hands. You may walk past a bakery, catch the smell of bread, and be reminded of your mother's love, but that aroma did not originate from her hands. It is merely a tangible reminder.

In the spiritual realm, however, you will no longer have a nose to smell your mother's bread, eyes to see her loving smile, ears to hear her say, *"I love you,"* a tongue to taste her homemade bread, or skin to feel her loving touch. According to the Talmud, these five senses will be wrapped into one unified sense. In the spirit, we will be able to smell, see, hear, taste, and feel *racham* love—all with the intensity of all five senses combined. It will be an experience of love never fully possible in this flesh—perhaps only at the moment our spirit begins to leave our corruptible body and becomes truly one with our heavenly Father. David understood this, which is likely why he said, *"I will racham you, Lord,"* instead of, *"I do racham you, Lord."*

So, what is it that Peter experienced in his final moments? I believe it was that *racham* love. In that moment, he was transported into a *tzim tzum*. This is a term I will describe in a later chapter. It is a sort of bubble between the natural and the supernatural world. Peter experienced this world and the spiritual realm simultaneously, allowing him to experience the full *racham* love of God. When he experienced it, he faced his last moments with joy and praise to God.

I recall when I was a student at Moody Bible Institute during a missionary conference. Various missionaries met with students in the dormitory. The men's dormitory, Culbertson Hall, has nineteen floors, and each floor has a lounge area. I remember a missionary who met with us in our lounge and told stories of his experiences on his particular mission field. He was serving in a country that had gone through a revolution, and at one point, he was arrested as a spy. He was placed in prison, and one day, they took him out to be shot. He and another prisoner, a French diplomat, were tied to a stack with their hands behind their backs, facing a squad of soldiers with rifles aimed at them. As the order was about to be given, the missionary whispered to the Frenchman, "I hope they aim at me and not you."

The Frenchman, already shaken, muttered, "Whhhhhhhy!"

The missionary calmly replied, "Because they are lousy shots, and they will miss me and hit you." He said, for some reason, the Frenchman did not find humor in that statement. Even when the rifles were shot and turned out to have blanks, the Frenchman collapsed, but the missionary only smiled.

In fact, the missionary said that what he really felt was great disappointment. At that moment, he was surrounded by an unspeakable, unexplainable love—so great that he could joke and laugh at the idea of dying because this love, this *racham* love, was far greater than life itself.

It is interesting that when it came time for Aaron to die, he, Moses, and his son Eleazar climbed to the top of a mountain. Wait a minute—a man is about to die, and he climbs a mountain? That doesn't sound like a man on his deathbed. Then something curious happened. After passing the garments of the high priest onto his son, Aaron calmly walked into a cave, laid down, and died. The way it reads in Hebrew, it sounds almost as if he passed on the garments and said, "Okay, I think I'm going to lay down and take a nap." Even more curious is that when all Israel heard of Aaron's death, they mourned for thirty days. Yet, there is no record that Moses, Aaron's brother, or Aaron's son Eleazar grieved or mourned.

Now let's take a look at Moses, who asked to see the glory of God. What is this glory? We don't fully know. The word *kabod* in Hebrew simply means heaviness, greatness, honor, or even stubbornness. These are not tangible things that you can see, hear, taste, or touch. Yet, this is what Moses wanted to experience—something that would allow him to know God more intimately. The word *know* in Hebrew is *yadah*, which conveys an intimate knowing. It is the same word used to describe sexual intimacy in a marriage relationship.

Who could have known God better than Moses? He was the one to whom God appeared in the burning bush, through whom God performed miracles, and whom He spoke to face-to-face, as one speaks to a friend. Yet Moses knew there was something more—something deeper. The closer Moses drew to God, the more he realized how little he truly knew Him. His spirit cried out to know God in the ultimate way God had created him to experience this intimacy.

Moses would later confirm this yearning by witnessing his brother's death. Something happened on that mountain when Aaron passed that was so glorious and wonderful that neither Moses, Aaron's brother, nor his son Eleazar mourned or grieved his death.

God told Moses He could not let him experience what he wanted because it would cause him to die. The Jewish sages teach that when Moses asked to see the glory of God, he was asking for it all. He wanted to experience the total, complete love of God—he wanted to know what that *racham* love truly was. But God said He could only give him a taste because if He gave him that full experience, Moses's spirit could no longer remain in his sinful, corrupt body. That physical body would die. The Jewish sages teach that if Moses actually saw, felt, heard, tasted, and touched the *racham* love of God, his spirit would have to leave his body, and once it was united with God, it would refuse to return. Moses's mission on Earth was not yet complete, so God could not allow him to leave his physical body. God did the only thing He could do without violating His laws— He gave him just a sample when Moses turned his back.

The words *striking dead* are an unfortunate translation. They hint at something tragic and horrible. It should instead be expressed as simply a transition from the physical realm to the realm of the spirit. Once the spirit is released from the flesh, it is free to be joined with the Spirit of God in a way that is not possible in a sinful, corrupt physical body. One day, we will have a new body—a resurrected body that is incorruptible—and we will be able to join with God, capable of experiencing full *racham* love.

The Jews call this passing from the flesh into the world of the spirit the *Divine Kiss*—a passing without pain, fear, or agony. If we are growing in our love for God and seeking to discover His heart, then, as Corrie ten Boom learned, when the time comes, we will have what we need. We will look at death with joy and praise on our lips, just like that missionary facing a firing squad.

Many Christians wonder how they will face death—would they be willing to die for the Lord? If you are seeking to grow in your love for God, to know His heart, and to seek first His kingdom and His righteousness, then when that time comes, you will not only have all you need but more than you could ever imagine. If it is a false alarm, as it was for that missionary, you will not be met with relief but rather disappointment over not continuing in that *tzim tzum*—that bubble of immense, glorious, unconditional love that God encapsulates you in during those final moments.

1. DEATH WHERE IS YOUR STING?

"O death, where [is] thy sting? O grave, where [is] thy victory?

The sting of death [is] sin; and the strength of sin [is] the law.

But thanks [be] to God, which giveth us the victory through our Lord Jesus Christ." (I Corinthians 15:55-57)

"And the Amorites, which dwelt in that mountain, came out against you, and chased you, as bees do, and destroyed you in Seir, [even] unto Hormah." (Deuteronomy 1:44)

"Too tired of living, too scared of dying." From *Ol' Man River* – Oscar Hammerstein II

I remember hearing I Corinthians 15:55 quoted as a child, and I shuddered. Death has a sting to it? For some reason, that expression haunted me. It made death sound like a painful experience. Why was Paul referring to death with a sting? I am not sure exactly what it was about the word *sting* that bothered me, but it never seemed quite right. Yet, every English translation I read uses the word *sting*. The word in Greek for *sting* is *kentron*, which means to prick, a sharp point, or to sting.

Many commentators believe Paul was quoting Hosea 13:14, *"I will ransom them from the power of the grave; I will redeem them from death: O death, I will be thy plagues; O grave, I will be thy destruction: repentance shall be hid from mine eyes."*

This verse seems to follow the same line of thought, except it says, *"O death, I will be thy plagues, O grave, I will be thy destruction."* Some claim Paul misquoted this verse, which would bring the inspiration of Scripture into question. Others suggest that *sting* and *plagues* essentially mean the same thing.

I turned to the Aramaic version of the Bible, Paul's native language, and found the word used for *sting* was *'aqats*, which conveys the idea of bending and twisting. It is an agricultural term for forcibly removing the fruit of a vine or tree by bending and twisting it. Rather than allowing the fruit to fall naturally, the harvester forces it off the branch. This definition might connect to our study verse if used as a verb. However, in this passage, it is a noun. As a noun, *'aqats* is used to describe the stinger of a bee, which twists and bends when removing its stinger, often resulting in the bee's death. This brings to mind Deuteronomy 1:44: *"And the Amorites, which dwelt in that mountain, came out against you, and chased you, as bees do."*

I recall a personal experience when my brother and I co-directed a summer camp for inner-city children, with a session for 6-8-year-olds. I played the role of "bad cop" to maintain discipline and quickly earned the nickname "Mr. Meany." At the start of the session, I laid down the camp rules, one of which was never to enter the woods without a counselor. Violators would receive up to five checks on my clipboard. I never explained the consequences of the checks, as there were none; the mere idea of receiving one was deterrent enough.

One camper, older and bigger than the rest, ignored the rule. She led her entire cabin group into the woods without a counselor. Suddenly, I heard screaming and saw the girls running out, followed by a swarm of bees. The bees chased them all the way back to camp and began attacking everyone. Later, as the camp nurse tended to their bee stings, the girls accused me, "Mr. Meany," of sending the bees after them for breaking the rules. It reminded me of how God is often blamed for things He did not cause.

In Deuteronomy 1:44, if you aren't familiar with bees, you might think the verse means the Amorites simply chased the Israelites like a swarm. However, Rashi, a medieval Jewish commentator, noted that bees lose their stinger and die after stinging, much like honeybees. He likened this to the Amorites, who, like bees, were destined to die after losing their sting. Similarly, for believers in Jesus, Paul teaches that the sting of death is sin. But if Jesus died to remove sin, then death loses its sting. Once we die, the enemy loses his ability to harass or tempt us. Sin brings death, but death leads us to life with Jesus and freedom from the enemy's grasp.

In I Corinthians 15:55-57, *'aqats* as a noun fits better as "stinger" rather than "sting." The verse could read: *"O death, where is your stinger?"*

The stinger is death's tool, a weapon that separates sinners from God. However, for believers, our sins are forgiven, and death no longer separates us from God. Instead, it unites us with Him in the final consummation of our relationship. For believers, there is no painful sting, no suffering, no fear, or terror in death. It becomes the culmination of our union with God. The enemy, stripped of his stinger, cannot accuse us or prevent our eternal union with Jesus. Death transforms from a source of fear to a joyous moment, the *Divine Kiss*.

Still, even believers may fear death for various reasons. I remember a passenger I drove to dialysis three times a week. Though wheelchair-bound and partially paralyzed, he always shared joyful stories. One day, he confessed he wanted to die, feeling like a burden and unable to contribute to society. However, he added, "But it would break my wife's heart if I died. So, I just keep on living for her sake."

I have many passengers on my disability bus who face extreme physical challenges, yet they keep visiting their healthcare providers and continue living. Many tell me the same thing: "God is keeping me alive for a reason." Once a person loses their reason for living, they often don't last long on this earth. I've had more than one elderly woman riding my bus say to me, "I just want to live long enough to attend my granddaughter's wedding." Even that little spark of hope keeps a person going.

I once knew a family friend who spent his entire adult life working for a major corporation. Right after military service, he began working for the company, establishing and maintaining its mainframe computer system. He traveled the world, troubleshooting computer problems wherever his corporation had a presence. He earned excellent money, which he invested wisely. Living a very frugal lifestyle in a small one-bedroom house near his job, he never bought a new car, instead repairing his old one until it was no longer feasible. Only then would he purchase an inexpensive used vehicle. He never married and had virtually no outside interests beyond his job.

At age 62, like many corporations at the time, his employer transitioned from mainframe systems to personal computers. His job became obsolete, and he was considered too old to retrain in a new field, so the company forced him into retirement. I didn't see him for almost a year after his retirement, and when I did, I was shocked by the change. He was only 63 years old but looked like he was in his eighties. A year later, he passed away. There was nothing seriously wrong with his health; he had substantial savings and retirement income to enjoy the finer things in life. Yet, he simply died. His body seemed to shut down because he had lost his purpose for living—it was as if he willed himself to die.

For many people, the fear of dying stems from the thought of leaving loved ones behind or not fulfilling their purpose in life. For others, death might seem preferable to the life they are forced to endure, yet, as Oscar Hammerstein II wrote in *Ol' Man River,* they feel "too tired of living, too scared of dying." There is often a natural fear of the unknown. For some, this fear becomes a terror they avoid at all costs, clinging to life desperately. Others may suffer from depression—a mental illness that leaves them wanting to die but too afraid to do so. These individuals live in a state of passive suicide that may eventually lead to active suicide. They live without hope, in mental anguish and torment, until the end comes—whether by their own hand or natural causes.

Socrates once said, "No one knows whether death may not even turn out to be the greatest blessing of human beings. And yet people fear it as if they knew for certain it is the greatest evil." Even those who profess a belief in an afterlife often harbor a fear of death. As Socrates suggested, the fear of death persists, even for those convinced that heaven awaits them.

Perhaps this is why God compares the transition from this life to eternity with Him as the consummation of a marriage. Marriage is a time of joy, celebration, and the rejoicing of two people discovering a deep, special love for each other. The consummation of that marriage is viewed as the fulfillment of great anticipation and excitement. This is likely why the Jewish sages refer to the transition from this world to the next as the *Divine Kiss.*

In ancient times, as even today, a bride would leave her father's home and family to join her husband in a completely new life. Jewish teachers say that passing through the marriage canopy symbolizes being "born again." Just as birth marks the beginning of one life, marriage marks the start of a new life—a life built around one's spouse and the family they create together. This profound change is celebrated with great rejoicing because it fulfills the deep human desire to belong entirely to another person and to be one with them.

So it is with death: it fulfills the soul's desire to be joined with its Creator, to become one with Him in love and peace. Why, then, do we fear death? Why is it considered an evil? For many, it is not.

D.L. Moody, on his deathbed, remarked, "Is this dying? Why, this is bliss. There is no valley. I have been within the gates. Earth is receding; Heaven is opening; God is calling, I must go." Moody often preached that "Death may be the King of Terrors, but Jesus is the King of Kings." Clearly, when Moody faced death, there was no fear, no terror, and no agony. He saw and experienced something extraordinary—a *Divine Kiss*. Before that final moment, it seems he was embraced by God in a *Divine Hug*. Just as a bride kisses her new husband during their wedding ceremony, Moody experienced the joy of leaving his old life behind to begin a new, exciting life with Someone he loved more than life itself. For Moody, as for millions of believers throughout history, death was not the end but a blissful beginning—a *Divine Hug* followed by a *Divine Kiss*.

When I was in high school, I played football. I wasn't very good at it and didn't enjoy the game, but I played due to outside pressure. I didn't want to be labeled a quitter, so I pushed through, despite the lack of joy. However, my heart wasn't in the sport, and before games, I would get physically sick with fear. While others called it "normal pre-game nerves," I suspected my fear was different.

Once, I met Randy Hundley, a professional baseball player for the Chicago Cubs. I asked him if he ever felt fear before a game. He replied, "I don't know if it's fear. I feel anxious and excited. There's a dread of the unknown—wondering if I'll make a mistake or let my teammates down. But it's not fear. If it were, I'd avoid playing. Instead, I feel challenged, eager to succeed, and thrilled by the opportunity to celebrate victory with my team."

That conversation confirmed my suspicions—what I felt was fear, not excitement. I cared only about avoiding personal embarrassment, not about victory or my teammates. I played out of obligation, not joy.

Perhaps this is the difference between a believer and a non-believer facing death. Believers pass from this world with the confidence of a mission accomplished. They have no fear of mistakes, failures, or sins because the sting of death has been removed by Jesus. Their only desire is to hear their Savior's reassurance: *"Well done, thou good and faithful servant."* (Matthew 25:23), followed by the *Divine Kiss* that marks their entrance into eternity.

2. THE MOUTH OF THE LORD

"So Moses the servant of the LORD died there in the land of Moab, according to the word of the LORD." (Deuteronomy 34:5)

When Moses died, Scripture does not say he simply died; rather, it states that he died by the word of the Lord. What does it mean to die by the word of the Lord? Does the Lord say, "Die," and then it happens? In Hebrew, *"the word of the Lord"* is *al pei Adonai,* which literally means *"by the mouth of the Lord."* Of course, God does not have a physical mouth—this is an anthropomorphism, a literary device attributing human characteristics, traits, emotions, or intentions to God. God is spirit and does not have eyes, ears, a nose, or a mouth. However, we use these human-like descriptions to better understand His nature and character.

For Moses to die *by the mouth of the Lord* has led most translators to interpret this phrase as God speaking certain words that resulted in Moses' death. However, Jewish sages interpret this anthropomorphism differently: they see it as God leaning down from heaven to end Moses' life with a soft, gentle kiss.

The Hebrew word for *mouth* is *pei,* which means the mouth as well as an opening or entryway. A mouth, as an opening, provides access to the interior of the body. From this perspective, one might say God ended Moses's life by *swallowing him up,* symbolizing Moses entering the very being of God. This could represent becoming part of God or having an intimate, eternal, and personal connection with Him.

Jewish sages teach that the *mouth of God* symbolizes a kiss. A kiss is one of the most intimate physical expressions, yet it stops short of a sexual relationship. Between lovers, a kiss often precedes deeper intimacy. Similarly, in Genesis 2:24, the Bible describes the union of husband and wife: *"Therefore shall a man leave his father and his mother, and shall cleave unto his wife: and they shall be one flesh."*

While in our corrupt physical bodies, we cannot fully become one with God. God cannot be joined with corruption. However, through the blood of Jesus, our souls are made incorruptible. Once our souls leave our bodies, we are free to be joined with God in the ultimate expression of intimacy.

In Deuteronomy 34:5, we are told that Moses died *"according to the mouth of God."* The word *according* translates from the Hebrew word *'al*, a preposition with numerous possible meanings, such as *upon, above, over,* or *according to.* This suggests Moses did not die *because of* the mouth of God, but *according to* it. Some translators interpret this as Moses dying according to the *word of the Lord.* But if that is the case, why assume the word spoken was, *"Die?"* Why not assume the word was, *"Love?"* Moses died according to the *racham* love of God.

Consider the picture of a husband and wife on their wedding night. In *devekut*—a loving embrace—they shut out the world, as if only the two of them exist. The husband then gives his bride a soft, gentle kiss, whispering, *"I love you."* By his word, she submits herself entirely to him in the sacred intimacy of marriage. Similarly, when God says to us, *"I love you,"* while holding us in a divine embrace, our souls cannot resist. They leave our bodies and become one with God.

At what point do we die? Can we even call this experience *dying?* Is God commanding us to die, or is He *loving us to death* in the most literal sense? Just as a bride may feel nervous before her wedding, her fears disappear with that first kiss after the ceremony. Yet, that kiss is not the consummation of the marriage. It is the culmination of love that causes the soul to leave the body.

I am often haunted by a story I heard as a child about a woman deeply involved in the occult. She had a spirit guide and believed she was serving God as a devoted Christian. On her deathbed, surrounded by loved ones, she said, *"Oh, I see my spirit guide coming for me."* Then, she let out a terrifying scream and died. I doubt she received a *Divine Kiss.* Whoever or whatever she had served during her life was not the God of heaven.

In contrast, I think of my father's passing. He spent three days unresponsive in a hospital bed, surrounded by family. On the third day, a hospice care worker informed us he had passed away. He died peacefully, without agony or pain. I was amazed at the sense of peace that settled over me and my family. I believe my father was receiving a *Divine Hug* during those three days, followed by a *Divine Kiss.* When God whispered to him, *"I love you,"* his soul left his body. Like Moses, he died *ai pei Adonai—*by the mouth of the Lord, the *Divine Kiss.*

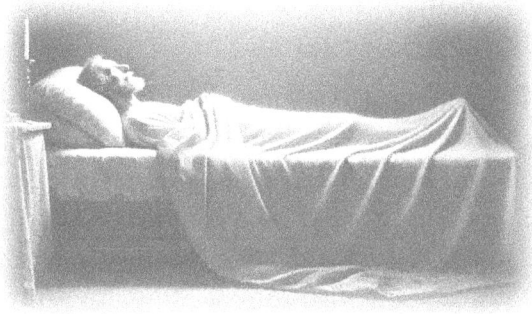

3. WHAT IS DEATH?

And all flesh died that moved upon the earth, both of fowl, and of cattle, and of beast, and of every creeping thing that creepeth upon the earth, and every man: (22) All in whose nostrils was the breath of life, of all that was in the dry land, died. (Genesis 7:21-22)

"When Jesus heard that, he said, This sickness is not unto death, but for the glory of God, that the Son of God might be glorified thereby." (John 11:4)

"Then said Jesus unto them plainly, Lazarus is dead." (John 11:14)

In Hebrew, we find that there are two words for death. The most common word is *muth,* which means to die, the end of life, or a corpse. This word is used in Genesis 7:22, which tells us that when the flood of Noah came upon the earth, all in whose nostrils was the breath of life, of all that was in the dry land, *muth*—died. However, in the prior verse (Genesis 7:21), we learn that all flesh that moved upon the earth, both the fowl and the cattle and all creeping things, and every man, *gava'*—died.

Gava' is also translated as death. Why does the writer use two different words for death? How can there be two different words for death? Dead is dead, right? Rabbis teach that there are no true synonyms in Hebrew. If two words seem to mean the same thing, there must be a difference between them, even if it is subtle—a small nuance, but a difference nonetheless.

Rabbi Samson Hirsch, a 19th-century linguist and Hebrew master, teaches that *gava'* describes a death without any suffering. That sounds like the definition of a *Divine Kiss*. Rashi, the medieval Jewish commentator and Hebrew master, associates *gava'* specifically with the death of the righteous.

Using *gava'* for death in Genesis 7:21 opens the door to some very interesting thoughts. For one thing, the animals and birds did not suffer when they died in the flood. Animals, having no free will, are not accountable for sin; they are innocent. It stands to reason that God would not cause them to suffer when they died in the flood. Similarly, we find that some *adams*—human beings—also died without suffering. Drowning is often described as one of the worst ways to die: the body screams for air, and when you finally take a breath, you inhale water, choking until your body expires from lack of oxygen. Yet, this passage suggests that some humans did not experience the agony of drowning.

The word *gava'* seems to point to the moment of death itself. Perhaps, at the moment of the flood, many humans acknowledged God and surrendered to Him, experiencing a painless transition into eternity. This could be likened to the two criminals crucified alongside Jesus. One repented in his last moments, while the other mocked Him. Similarly, during the flood, some may have repented at the last moment, receiving the *Divine Kiss,* while others cursed God and died in agony.

When we turn to the New Testament, the story of Lazarus is particularly intriguing. In John 11:4, after learning that Lazarus was sick, Jesus tells His disciples that the sickness would not lead to death. Yet, just ten verses later, He plainly states that Lazarus had died. This apparent contradiction has been a source of confusion for many. Critics argue that Jesus should have been discredited as a false prophet for predicting that Lazarus would not die, only to later admit that he had. To reconcile this, some Bible commentators suggest that Jesus was speaking metaphorically or spiritually, rather than literally. Others propose that Jesus meant Lazarus would not experience permanent death. All these interpretations have merit, but they often feel like attempts to explain away a contradiction.

The Greek text offers additional insight. Both words used for death stem from the same root, but the first instance uses *thanaton,* which could refer to either spiritual or physical death. The second instance uses *apoth-*

nesko, with *apo* meaning "to be separated" or "away from." This suggests that when Jesus first said Lazarus's sickness would not end in death, He might have been referring to spiritual death. The second reference likely points to physical death. Another possible interpretation is that Jesus was saying Lazarus's death would not be a permanent state.

The Aramaic text provides even more precision. The first time Jesus speaks of death, He uses the word *muth*—a noun cognate with the Hebrew *muth.* This would indicate a permanent state of death. However, the second time, Jesus uses *mith,* a verb in the *Pael* inflection and perfect form. The *Pael* form conveys a result, and the perfect form indicates a completed action, but not necessarily a permanent state. Jesus was essentially saying that Lazarus would die, but it would not be a permanent state. This aligns with the Greek rendering of the text.

In John 11:3, we see something else worth noting: *"Therefore his sisters sent unto him, saying, Lord, behold, he whom thou lovest is sick."*

The word for love here is *racham.* Typically, Mary and her sister would have used *chav,* the most common word for love and the ultimate love one can experience in the flesh. However, their use of *racham* suggests a deeper, spiritual love beyond the physical realm. It implies they recognized the divinity of Jesus and His power to heal. By using *racham,* they were not merely asking Jesus to visit an old friend but to heal him through His divine power.

When Jesus explained that Lazarus's death was not permanent, He added that it was for the glory of God so that the Son of God might be glorified. The word *glorified* in Aramaic is *shavach,* meaning *to rise in value* or *to praise.* In the *Ithpael* form—similar to the *Hithpael* in Hebrew—it is reflexive, meaning it could be rendered as: *"So the Son of God may glorify Himself,"* or *"raise the value of Himself in the eyes of others."* Jesus was essentially saying that He would perform this resurrection to reveal His divine nature.

Finally, Jesus plainly states, *"Lazarus is dead."* Here, He uses the word *mith* rather than *muth.* While both mean "death," *mith* is used as a verb in the *Pael* form, showing a result. The word *plainly* in Aramaic is *pashaq,* meaning *to be simple, clear, or straightforward.* Jesus was clearly saying, "Lazarus is physically dead, but this is not a permanent state."

Something troubling about this exchange is the disciples' lack of understanding. Jesus speaks in cryptic terms about life and death, and it seems He eventually grows frustrated. It's as if He throws up His hands and says: "He's dead already, okay? Don't you get it? I see death very differently than you do. How could I have created beings so limited that they can't understand death like I do?"

I believe Jesus knew all along that the disciples could not see death as He saw it. He understood the limitations of our natural understanding, and until that moment when we pass from this life, we will not understand death as Jesus does. But I believe Jesus was doing with His disciples what He is doing with you and me, those who are born into His family through His shed blood. He gives us moments—special opportunities to experience His extreme loving presence, a taste of His *racham*—as much as He can show us, just as He did with Moses. These moments prepare us for that day when we pass from this body. When was the last time you were worshiping God and felt so caught up in His presence that you just wanted to stay that way forever? That feeling was God giving you a taste of what you will experience moments before you leave this world. However, what you felt is only a teaspoon of what is to come. You are in for something far, far greater.

God had to instill in us a natural instinct to resist death, to fear it. Otherwise, as soon as life became challenging, we would simply say, "Hey, I'm out of here. Enough of this crappy existence when I could be passing through pearly gates and walking streets of gold. No more bad backs, no aging, no suffering from viruses—I'm going to opt for eternal peace and tranquility." Imagine standing at the edge of a cliff, ready to jump, when suddenly that natural fear of death kicks in. You feel that surge of, "Uh, maybe I'll just stick it out and see what God has prepared." God instilled the fear of death in us to prevent us from making an early exit. We are sent to this earth with a mission, and the challenges required to fulfill that mission can often feel overwhelming. In moments of weakness, it would be tempting to opt out if an easy exit were available. Moses himself had one of those moments of weakness and asked God to let him experience the *Divine Kiss*. However, if God had allowed it, Moses's spirit would have decided to leave his body permanently. So, God gave him only a "peck on the cheek."

I recall hearing the testimony of a man who was clinically dead for fifteen minutes. His spirit left his body, and he spoke with Jesus face to face. His testimony was so powerful and filled with such deep love for Jesus that I couldn't question the reality of his experience. However, Jesus told him he had to return to his body, which he obediently did. Despite the love he expressed for Jesus, I could sense a deep yearning for more—something beyond what he had experienced when he met Jesus outside his body. His *Divine Kiss* was only a "peck on the cheek," leaving him wanting more. That testimony was given over fifty years ago, and I am certain that by now, he has experienced the full *Divine Kiss,* fulfilling the deep yearning I sensed from his testimony.

As we walk with Jesus, just as His disciples did, He uses various experiences to prepare us, much like raising Lazarus from the dead. Gradually and lovingly, Jesus chips away at our natural fear of death, replacing it with a deeper desire to fulfill our earthly mission. This desire becomes our motivation to remain in our physical bodies until our time comes. When Jesus finally says, "Time to go, old friend—your chariot of fire awaits!" we will be ready and equipped for the journey in ways we cannot yet imagine.

As I approach the twilight years of my journey on earth, I find that my fear of death is fading, replaced by a growing sense of anticipation. With each passing year, I feel myself drawing closer to what the old songwriter called the "great getting-up morning." I feel God chipping away at my fear of death, revealing the true longing of my heart: to experience that *Divine Kiss.*

In my quiet moments, alone with my Savior, I feel His arms around me. It reminds me of when I was eight years old, away from home for the first time at summer camp. I woke one morning with a deep yearning to be home in my own bed. The activities of the day eventually distracted me, but throughout the day, memories of my parents and the time we spent together would flood my mind. I would feel that emptiness and longing again. One day, while sitting on a log, my camp counselor, a teenager himself, asked what was wrong. I told him I missed my father and the times we spent fishing together. He patted me on the head and said, "I know how you feel. I get homesick sometimes too." It was then that I realized: I was homesick.

Now, as I approach the later years of my life, I find myself sitting on that proverbial log again, thinking about my Heavenly Father and feeling the same homesickness I felt as a child. With each passing year, this longing grows stronger.

I vividly remember an experience when I was seven years old. My family attended a sportsman's convention at the old Chicago Amphitheater. While exploring the booths, I became engrossed in a demonstration. When I looked up, my parents and brother were gone. My seven-year-old mind panicked. I felt utterly lost and alone. Though I tried to enjoy the convention, all I could think about was finding my family. Then, in the distance, I saw my father. I ran straight into his open arms, where he hugged me tightly and said, "We've been looking all over for you." In that moment, my fear, loneliness, and longing disappeared, replaced by overwhelming joy.

As I get older, I feel that same sense of loneliness and longing to be reunited with my Heavenly Father. I know that when the day comes, when I see Him in the distance, my spirit will leave my body and run to Him. He will embrace me with a *Divine Hug* and say, "I've been waiting a long time for you." I can only imagine the joy of that moment, knowing it will be far greater than anything I've ever experienced. That moment will be the *Divine Kiss.*

Let's return to the story of Lazarus.

> *These things said he: and after that he saith unto them, Our friend Lazarus sleepeth; but I go, that I may awake him out of sleep. (12) Then said his disciples, Lord, if he sleep, he shall do well. (13) Howbeit Jesus spake of his death: but they thought that he had spoken of taking of rest in sleep.* (John 11:11-13)

Jews of the first century understood that the word for sleep was often used as a euphemism—a gentler, less offensive term. Just as today we avoid saying "death" and use words like "passing" or "passed away," the term for sleep was similarly used. However, the disciples did not grasp this nuance because Jesus assured them that Lazarus's sickness would not result in death (*muth* in Aramaic). So, when Jesus said Lazarus was sleeping, they thought He meant literal sleep.

The word in Aramaic that Jesus used in verse 11 for sleep is *shakav*. This is not the standard Aramaic word for sleep. This word is particularly interesting because it can mean actual sleep, death, or, in a third sense, intimacy. Specifically, it is sometimes used to describe a man lying with another man, though not necessarily implying intercourse, but rather a deep expression of intimacy.

With such varied meanings, it's no wonder the disciples misunderstood what Jesus was referencing. Reading this passage in English makes it easy to make the same mistake as the disciples, as it might appear that Jesus was a false prophet. He predicted that Lazarus would not die (*muth*), but just eleven verses later, we learn that Lazarus did indeed die (*muth*).

In verse 11, Jesus says that Lazarus *shakav*—that is, he is sleeping in intimacy. The disciples then respond that if he is sleeping, he does well. They use the Aramaic word *damak,* which is still not the usual word for sleep in Aramaic (*yashan*). Neither Jesus nor the disciples use *yashan*. Instead, *damak* refers to a healing kind of sleep.

In ancient times, determining death was challenging. Much like today, people might fall into a coma and fail to respond to physical stimulation. If someone did not respond, they were often considered dead, even if they still had a heartbeat and were breathing.

The Greeks, a scientifically inclined culture, understood that if there was a heartbeat and breathing, a person was still alive. However, without modern medical science, they could not nourish a comatose person intravenously. Thus, individuals in comas would usually die within a few days from dehydration or starvation. In that climate, someone in a coma could typically only survive three days without water.

In the first century, when a person was declared dead, their body was placed in a cave for three days. If they didn't awaken within those three days, they were deemed truly dead. This tradition explains why Jesus waited two days before going to see Lazarus. By the time He arrived in Bethany, enough time had passed for Lazarus to die from dehydration if he were in a coma, removing any doubt about his death. This also explains why Jesus Himself remained in the tomb for three days before His resurrection—to dispel any question about whether He was genuinely dead.

The disciples used the word *damak* because they believed Lazarus was in a coma—a state considered a trance-like condition. In Greek medical tradition, healing chambers were often located in caves. A sick individual would be given a potion to induce a trance-like state, where it was believed the gods would reveal the nature of their illness and its cure. Archaeologists have found such chambers, including antechambers where priests would hide and speak to the patient, pretending to be gods. The Aramaic word *damak* reflects this understanding of sleep as a state of healing or recovery.

However, this doesn't resolve the apparent contradiction. In verse 4, Jesus says the sickness will not lead to death (*muth*), but in verse 13, we learn that Lazarus did *muth*—die. One way to reconcile this is to consider that Lazarus received the *Divine Kiss*. Jesus was making a distinction between spiritual death and physical death.

The word *muth*, in its root form, refers to the separation of the soul from the physical body. For an unbeliever, this separation results in eternal disconnection from God—spiritual death. For a believer, however, the soul is joined with its Creator, entering a supernatural life of intimacy with God. This is not spiritual death, as it involves no separation from God. Instead, Jesus uses the word *shakav*, referring to an intimate union with God.

This suggests that the *Divine Kiss* occurs before the physical death is complete, emphasizing the soul's transition into life with God rather than its departure from the body. Lazarus's body died, but before his soul left his body, he experienced the *Divine Kiss*, leaving him unaware of or indifferent to his physical death.

The use of *shakav* teaches us that, as believers, we will not be conscious of our passing. We may lie there with a smile on our faces, unconcerned about what we are leaving behind, completely enveloped in the loving arms of God. Nothing else will matter.

4. BENNY'S A COME HOME

For I am already being poured out as a drink offering, and the time of my departure is at hand. (5) But you be watchful in all things, endure afflictions, do the work of an evangelist, fulfill your ministry. (7) I have fought a good fight, I have finished my course, I have kept the faith: (8) Henceforth there is laid up for me a crown of righteousness, which the Lord, the righteous judge, shall give me at that day: and not to me only, but unto all them also that love his appearing. (II Timothy 4:5-8)

This *Divine Kiss* starts to come upon us at various times. The Apostle Paul began to experience it many months before his actual passing when he said: *"I am already being poured out as a drink offering, and my time of departure is at hand."* Paul was more and more beginning to feel a taste of that *racham* love.

Earlier, I spoke about Peter, where Jesus told him in John 18:28-29:

Verily, verily, I say unto thee, When thou wast young, thou girdedst thyself, and walkedst whither thou wouldest: but when thou shalt be old, thou shalt stretch forth thy hands, and another shall gird thee, and carry thee whither thou wouldest not. This He spoke, signifying by what death he would glorify God. And when He had spoken this, He said to him, 'Follow Me.'

What did all this talk of being young, girding yourself, and then getting old with another girding you have to do with the death by which Peter would glorify God?

Like many of us, we can talk with much bravado about how we would die for the sake of Jesus. But in our quiet moments, even someone like Peter, when faced with the possibility of suffering for Jesus, began to worry about his own survival and "chickened out." Just as Peter boldly told Jesus that he would die for Him, only to deny Him a few hours later when accused of being associated with Him—a connection that could have led to suffering or even death.

After the resurrection, Jesus and Peter had a discussion on the seashore. This experience must have been at the forefront of Peter's mind. He was likely not only ashamed of himself for denying Jesus but also questioning whether he could ever be of any use to Him again. Jesus assured Peter that while his faith was still young, it would grow stronger. As he grew in his knowledge and relationship with God, Peter would become more confident, bolder, and willing to face death. He would no longer avoid death out of fear. Instead, something else would gird him: a longing to fulfill his mission and purpose in life, knowing that if he did, he could face his Lord unashamed.

History records that Peter faced his final moments with unspeakable courage. Courage, by definition, means overcoming fear. By the time Peter faced his death, he likely had no fear at all. He was ready—his mission was accomplished, and he could face his Lord unashamed. Jesus surely embraced him and said: *"Well done, thou good and faithful servant. Now let's get on with the true purpose of your existence and share in this abiding racham love."*

As I write this, I am well into the seventh decade of my life. This old body struggles just to get out of bed each morning. Some mornings, I sit alone in my office, trying to read God's Word. I bow my head and ask God why He is keeping me here—why He doesn't just take me home. I'm certainly not doing much good for anyone. I can't minister like I used to. I can't even pick myself up, so how am I supposed to lift someone else? How can I bring the joy of the Lord to others when I'm struggling just to maintain what little joy I have?

It's during these moments that I think of a story my father used to tell me as a child.

My father was eighteen years old when World War II broke out. Like many young men, he joined the military, training to defend his country. My father told me about a young man he befriended during basic training named Benny. Benny, like my father, grew up on a small farm in the hills of Missouri. He lived with his parents, a little sister, and a kid brother. Benny spent his days farming, hunting, and providing for his family. It was the only life he knew until one day, he received a telegram from Uncle Sam—the one that starts with the word, "Greetings."

Benny, just a young teenager, left his loving home and found himself in the foreign, unfamiliar environment of the U.S. Army. Don't get me wrong—Benny was an excellent soldier. Growing up on a farm, Benny was in excellent physical condition, unlike many urban draftees. He was an expert marksman and knew how to take orders, having been raised in a God-fearing home. But Benny had one flaw: he was homesick. He would walk around camp with my father and say, "Floyd, I miss my family. I miss my father, mother, sister, and kid brother. I've got to see them." My dad would try to encourage him, saying, "Listen, Benny, just hang in there. You're doing a good job. In a few weeks, we'll finish basic training, and you'll get a pass to go home and visit your family." But Benny couldn't wait.

One morning, during roll call, Benny's name was called, but there was no response. No one could find him. My father, however, knew. He knew Benny had gone home.

My father did the right thing. He went to the base chaplain, explained the situation, and the chaplain took him to the commanding officer (CO). My father told the CO about Benny: how he was a good, talented, and faithful soldier who was just a young boy from a loving family and deeply homesick. The Army went to Benny's home, picked him up, and brought him back. My understanding is that the CO backdated a special pass for Benny and covered up the whole affair. Perhaps the CO missed his own family and understood Benny's situation. Whatever the reason, Benny wasn't severely punished. Instead, he was allowed to rejoin his unit and complete basic training.

One night, just before lights out, my dad went to Benny's bunk and asked: "Hey, Benny? Did you make it? Did you make it home?" Benny's face lit up with a big smile, his eyes glowing as he said: "Floyd, when I crossed that last hill, I looked down into the valley and saw our little farmhouse. Smoke was coming out of the chimney, and I knew my mother and sister were cooking dinner. I looked out over the fields and saw my dad and kid brother repairing a fence. My kid brother was the first to see me. He began jumping up and down, shouting: 'Dad, it's Benny! Benny's a come home! Benny's a come home!'" Benny continued, "My whole family came out to greet me." Of course, the next day, the Army came and took him back.

My dad usually ended the story there, but I often imagined what that homecoming was like. I pictured Benny and his father sitting on the porch that evening after the rest of the family had gone to bed. I imagined his father saying something like this: "It's great to have you home, son, but you have to go back. Your country needs you. Your family is depending on you. And I'm counting on you. I know it's hard—I fought in the first war, and I know how hard it is. But this war will end, and when it does, you can come home to stay."

Well, that wise CO was right not to be harsh on Benny, for Benny made a fine soldier. He landed with my father on Omaha Beach during D-Day. He fought in France under General Patton. Benny received a Purple Heart and a Bronze Star. He was promoted to the rank of Staff Sergeant. Yes, Benny was indeed a hero; he served his country well. The war ended, and Benny was allowed to go home with an honorable discharge. When Benny crossed that last hill and looked into the valley, this time his kid brother began to shout: "Dad, it's Benny! Benny's a come home! He's come home to stay. And Dad, look, look at those medals, those stripes! Benny's a hero, he sure enough is a hero, ain't he, Dad?" Once again, his whole family came out to greet him. This time his father hugged Benny and said, "You did good, son. You did good. I'm proud of you. Now you can come home. You can come home to stay."

You know what I believe Benny did? He took those medals off his chest and gave them to his father, saying, "Dad, I know I earned these in Europe, but they really belong to you. You were the one who taught me how to use a rifle, how to survive, and when I couldn't go on, when I felt I just didn't have the ability to complete my mission, you were the one who encouraged me to continue."

How many of us have felt like Benny? How many of us who know and love Jesus with all our hearts get a bit homesick for our heavenly home? How many of us have not even contemplated going absent without leave, like Benny?

But if we did such a thing, we know the Heavenly Father would greet us and say: *"It's great to have you home, but it just wasn't time. I need you down there. There are people I want to reach down there. My kingdom needs you. The church is depending on you. And once more, I am counting on you. I know it's hard. I walked that earth Myself; I know how hard it is. But one day the war will be over, and you can come home. You can come home to stay."*

No longer would there be the fear of death—only the fear of not fulfilling our purpose and mission on this earth. That sense of mission and purpose is what will motivate us. It's what motivated Peter to stay for the duration and not seek an early exit. Then, when our war is over, when our mission is accomplished, we will be allowed to cross that last hill. Waiting for us will be our Heavenly Father, who will greet us and hug us, saying: *"Well done, thou good and faithful servant."* Or, in more modern terms, *"You done good, and I'm proud of you."*

But note what Paul tells us in II Timothy 4:8: *"…laid up for me is a crown of righteousness."*

In ancient times, warriors were given crowns to wear rather than medals. Sometimes, a king would remove a precious stone from his own crown and give it to a particularly special warrior. These crowns are akin to the medals a soldier receives for distinguished service. The Bible tells us we earn crowns here on earth, just as a warrior earns medals. There is the crown of life and other crowns. I'm sure all of us have at least a Purple Heart. I don't know about you, but whatever I have, I plan to take those crowns—those medals—and give them to my Heavenly Father, saying: "Father, I know I earned these on earth, but really, You were the one who gave me the ability to earn them. You were the one who equipped and strengthened me. Then, during those times when I couldn't go on, when every step was just too painful, when I longed for an early exit, You walked with me. You carried me. No, Father, these rewards really belong to You."

One day, we will realize that it was all worth it—every heartache, every moment of suffering. Perhaps when we get to heaven, we'll find many others there because we chose to continue fighting the good fight and staying in for the duration.

But pay close attention, for even if the day of your passing is years from now, God is already beginning to prepare you. Years before Rusty Goodman, the well-known gospel singer and songwriter, learned he had terminal cancer, he wrote a song called *"Leavin' on My Mind."* This song spoke of how he was gradually losing his focus on this natural world and thinking of the day he would meet Jesus and leave this world behind.

God is preparing you, even now, for that *Divine Kiss.* It may be years away, but when that time comes, you will experience something more wonderful than anything you have ever known in your years of walking this earth.

5. ENTERING GOD'S RACHAM

For I am persuaded, that neither death, nor life, nor angels, nor principalities, nor powers, nor things present, nor things to come, (39) Nor height, nor depth, nor any other creature, shall be able to separate us from the love of God, which is in Christ Jesus our Lord. (Romans 8:38-39)

I recently returned from spending a week of silence living in a Benedictine Monastery down South. The residents of the monastery were of a Trappist order who live a contemplative life based on the Rule of St. Benedict. To ensure their compliance with this discipline, they live in silence, and any guest attending a week-long retreat must also practice silence.

As I sat in my little monastic room provided by the monastery, toward the end of my silent retreat, I began to contemplate returning to my job driving a disability bus and resuming my normal life. I found myself dreading my return and began thinking about what I dreaded the most. I had to admit it was people asking: "Well, how was it?" I didn't know how to answer. I had no visions, no revelations, no animals talking to me, no ten-foot angels in combat boots appearing before me. It was simply a time of prayer, meditation, and worship.

Well, there was one thing, though I hardly thought it was worth mentioning. I sort of *had it out* with God.

You see, I had just turned 73 years of age. Having driven a disability bus for many years, serving mostly senior citizens, I was discovering something that all of us who have entered the seventh decade of our lives have in common: we realize that we are cannon fodder for faith healers.

I watched a faith healer on YouTube, performing for an audience primarily made up of Baby Boomers like myself. He had a healing line of at least a dozen people, none appearing to be under seventy. As the faith healer passed by each one, offering blessings, he suddenly stopped as if receiving a revelation. He waved his hand over the group and said: "Someone here has a blood sugar problem, someone has a heart condition, a bad back."

Now, anyone over the age of seventy would not find this particularly prophetic. I personally would have been impressed if he had said: "Why, none of you have a blood sugar problem, a heart condition, or a bad back!" That would have been truly prophetic—and a miracle to boot. An audience of senior citizens is like a candy store for faith healers. Call out any ailment, and odds are someone will cry out: "Why, that's me! How could he have known? Such an anointed prophet!"

When you're in your seventies and a faith healer calls out an ailment, you simply pull out your wallet with your Medicare card and prescription list and go down the line. Odds are you'll find that ailment somewhere on your list.

My point isn't to belittle faith healers. I mean, at this age, you have good days and bad days. A faith healer can get your adrenaline flowing, giving you a good day. But it also reminds you that the clock is ticking, and the sands of time are running out. You develop a profound spiritual insight: one day—perhaps very soon—you're really going to die.

As I sat in my little room at the Abbey, I cried out to God: "My time left on this earth is so short, and I have accomplished so little in my life. I don't know what to ask for; I don't know how to pray. There is something deep inside me that feels like fear, but I don't know what it is. Just one thing, Lord—that's all I'm asking for, just one thing because that's all I need to know. I need to know that I have accomplished my mission here on earth. But I don't know what it is. You know my heart better than I do. Please, give me that one thing I need in order to finish this race we call life and to know I have fulfilled my purpose."

I sat back, waiting for an angel to appear or for some divine revelation—perhaps even a phone call from the White House or the United Nations! Your fantasies can get wild at a time like this. But nothing happened.

Nothing, that is, except something common to all believers—those who have accepted Jesus Christ as their personal Savior. Those who are redeemed and purified by His blood.

You see, Jesus died on the cross for one primary purpose. Oh, there are many benefits to salvation: peace, joy, purpose in life, and, of course, eternity in heaven as part of the "retirement package." But these are all perks—not the real reason. The primary reason God desires to impart His salvation is to purify our hearts to receive His *racham* love—the love He longs to pour out on us.

God can impart His *ahav* love to anyone, regardless of their relationship with Him. But *racham* love is another level—a love only the redeemed can experience. It's a love we can only taste when we are in complete surrender to God, cleansed by the blood of Jesus. It is the love Moses experienced in the wilderness when God told him to turn his back as His glory (*racham* love) passed by.

We experience this taste of *racham* love at various moments in our lives when we most need it to keep moving forward. But when we face the greatest transition of all—death—that is when we will receive the full embodiment of *racham*.

At that moment, when I cried out to God for the one thing I needed most, He gave me what I've experienced many times in my walk with Him—a small taste of His love to help me push forward.

You know what I'm talking about. It's that love of God that envelops you. That warm, gentle, soothing presence of God. It's like trying to describe a Big Mac to someone. I can tell you how wonderful it tastes, but until you bite into one yourself, there's no way to fully understand.

Similarly, until you experience that spoonful taste of *racham*, you can't fully comprehend it, no matter how it's described to you.

For me, the greatest gift God gave in that moment was a little taste of *racham*. Like Moses, I found myself crying out, *"Oh, that I might see*

Your glory!" What I wanted most—what my heart longed for—was to see God's glory. But I realized that I could only experience *racham* in its fullness when I faced that final moment.

Apparently, God still has a mission for me here. All He could give me now was a little taste of *racham*, which only left me longing for more.

But when that time comes, I have the assurance Corrie ten Boom's father gave her: when I look into my heart, I will find the strength I need. For in my heart, I will find His *racham* love.

The Apostle Paul said in Romans 8:39 that nothing could separate him from the love of God through Christ Jesus. Interestingly, the word for love used here is *chav*—a cognate of the Hebrew word *ahav*. I've often wondered why Paul used a lesser word for love, instead of *racham*, to describe the unshakable bond of God's love.

Paul understood that he, like us, could not fully know *racham* love while in the flesh. What God gave him—and what He gave me in that mo-ment—was a good dose of *ahav* love, which is only a taste of *racham* love. I knew, no matter how wonderful it was, something even greater awaited me when He says those wonderful words: *"Well done, thou good and faithful servant."* When I enter into His presence, never to leave for eternity, I will find myself in the presence of true *racham* love.

From this moment on, every time I experience God's presence—His en-veloping love—I am now fully aware that something even greater awaits me: *racham,* or as I call it, the *Divine Kiss.* God can give me many things in the material and fleshly world. He can give me a house instead of an apartment, a healthy body, and great opportunities to speak and preach, but all those things will pass and are temporary.

Instead, He has given me something permanent—something that will be there when everything else fades away. He has given me the promise of His *ahav* love and the expectation of receiving His *racham* love, the *Divine Kiss,* after the battle is won.

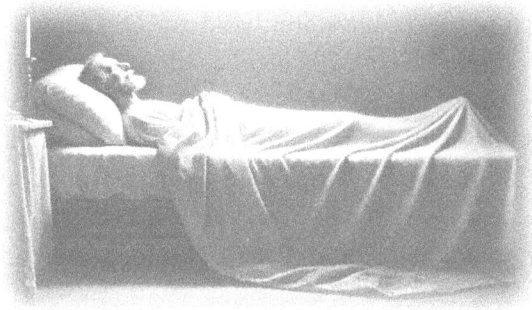

6. DID ENOCH REALLY DIE?

"And Enoch walked with God: and he was not; for God took him." (Genesis 5:24)

"By faith Enoch was translated that he should not see death; and was not found, because God had translated him: for before his translation he had this testimony, that he pleased God." (Hebrews 11:5)

I have often wondered why Genesis 5:24 is so cryptic about Enoch being taken by God to heaven without dying. Why couldn't the writer simply state it as Paul did in the Book of Hebrews, saying that he did not see death? Instead, we read: *"Enoch walked with God and he was not."* What is that supposed to mean? It sounds like Enoch just magically disappeared, except the next statement tells us that God took him. Took him where? Obviously, to heaven. Since his body disappeared and he was taken to heaven, why not just say so?

If this is the case—that God took Enoch to heaven without his dying—then this would mean his physical body took a journey through outer space (if we assume heaven is somewhere in outer space) or into some other dimension or alternative universe. How could a physical body exist in outer space? Maybe God created a little bubble filled with oxygen and other amenities needed for a body of flesh and blood to survive. Once in heaven, how was that body kept alive for four thousand years? Does heaven have an atmosphere? Will our spirits need oxygen to survive in heaven?

Then what did Enoch eat while in heaven? Practically everything we eat is something that was once alive and has died. Did Enoch exist for four thousand years on manna? If there is no death in heaven, then how does one get a square meal? Did God create a special bathroom just for Enoch, who would need to perform the same functions that all living creatures perform—the elimination of waste? Of course, he would need some sort of housing with heavy curtains to block out the light so he could sleep at night. Perhaps he has a mansion to live in. But then how did he not grow old, as all flesh does?

Maybe God took Enoch's consciousness and created an android, like in science fiction movies—an exact duplicate that would never die or grow old. Yet, if God did that, Enoch's original body would have had to die. Okay, God can do anything he wants and I am just getting too technical. But I'm just saying.

There are many who believe that Enoch did die and that his body was simply never found. After all, Hebrews 9:27 says, *"And as it is appointed unto men once to die, but after this the judgment."* Oddly, this verse, which declares that all humans made of flesh and blood must die, was written by the same man who, just a couple of chapters earlier, said Enoch did not see death. How do we reconcile this? One explanation is found in Revelation 11, which speaks of two witnesses who will appear during the tribulation period and will die. One of these witnesses, many believe, could be Enoch, finally dying a martyr's death after four thousand years.

Some commentators suggest that Enoch did die, but because he died at a relatively young age compared to other patriarchs, it might appear that God took him early. To prevent the perception that Enoch's early death was a sign of divine displeasure, Scripture avoids the offensive word "death" and instead uses a gentler phrase like "taken by God."

This explanation aligns with the *Targum,* which says *ameth yataeh yeya.* This phrase for death is in an *Aphel* form, which indicates that "God put him to death." The *Targum*—an Aramaic paraphrase of the Hebrew Bible that reflects the common understanding of the Old Testament among first-century Jews—interprets the phrase to mean that Enoch's death was directly caused by God. In this sense, Enoch didn't "die" in the tradition-al sense; he was simply "taken" by God, much like someone "going home to heaven."

But why did the Apostle Paul, who likely studied the *Targum,* say Enoch did not die? Actually, Paul does not necessarily state that Enoch did not die; he says Enoch did not *see* death. The Aramaic word for "see" is *ta'a,* which means to taste or experience. Paul may be suggesting that Enoch did not consciously experience death. If God gave him a *Divine Kiss,* Enoch would have been so completely focused on God and filled with God's *racham* love that he would not even have noticed the transition of his physical body into death.

In Genesis, the words "God took him" are used to describe Enoch's depar-ture. The Hebrew word for "took" is *laqach,* which is also used to describe the joyous announcement of a marriage: when a man announces that he has "taken" a bride. This word expresses joy and celebration. It would make sense for God to use such a word to describe Enoch's departure rather than a word that could imply punishment or sadness. Through *laqach,* God is essentially announcing that He was taking Enoch, His beloved servant, out of his earthly life and into a new and more fulfilled existence as His bride.

In Hebrews 11:5, Paul uses the Aramaic word *ashatani,* derived from the root word *shanah,* which refers to change or transformation. In its *Ethpael* form, the word becomes causative and intensive, emphasizing a complete change. God caused a complete transformation in Enoch so that he would not experience the pain, terror, or "sting" of death. In-stead, Enoch was translated into God's presence, bypassing the suffering usually associated with physical death.

Enoch was so favored by God because, as Genesis tells us, he "walked with God," and, as Paul notes, he "pleased God." The Aramaic word for "pleased" is *shaphar,* which means to be beautiful, like a bride adorning herself for her bridegroom. Enoch's life was in such harmony with God that God found him irresistible and longed to be one with him.

The Hebrew word for "walked" in Genesis 5:24 is *yitehaleka,* derived from the root word *halak.* It is in a *Hithpael* imperfect form with a *vav conversive,* which some linguists suggest adds the perfect to the imperfect, implying continuity. Thus, Enoch not only walked with God but continued to walk with Him all the way into eternity. Amos 3:3 says: *"Can two walk together, except they be agreed?"* Enoch walked in total agreement with God—in perfect harmony.

Psalm 37:23 states: *"The steps of a good man are ordered by the Lord: and he delighteth in his way."* The word for "steps" in Hebrew is *tsa'ad,* which also refers to an ankle bracelet or chain. In ancient cultures, slaves wore chains around their ankles to symbolize obedience to their master's will. Later, women adopted ornamental ankle bracelets to symbolize love and loyalty to their husbands. Enoch's "steps" being ordered by the Lord suggests that he wore a spiritual "ankle bracelet," signifying that he willingly followed wherever God led him. Ultimately, this path led Enoch to heaven, where he experienced the *Divine Kiss*—a transition without pain, terror, or the agony of death. He passed from this world into eternal life with God, wrapped in God's *racham* love.

7. NADAB AND ABIHU

And Nadab and Abihu, the sons of Aaron, took either of them his censer, and put fire therein, and put incense thereon, and offered strange fire before the LORD, which he commanded them not. So fire went out from the LORD and devoured them, and they died before the LORD. Then Moses said unto Aaron, This is it that the LORD spake, saying, I will be sanctified in them that come nigh me, and before all the people I will be glorified. And Aaron held his peace. (Leviticus 10:1-2)

"And the LORD spake unto Moses after the death of the two sons of Aaron, when they offered before the LORD, and died." (Leviticus 16:1)

Different translations render Leviticus 16:1—"And the LORD spake unto Moses after the death of the two sons of Aaron, when they offered before the LORD, and died"—quite differently. One translation says they died when they approached the Lord. The *New Living Bible* says they died when "they entered the Lord's presence and burned the wrong kind of fire." The *ESV* says they died when they drew near to the Lord. The *Amplified Bible* says they died when they (irreverently) approached the presence of the Lord. The *Douay* (Catholic) Bible says they were slain upon their offering of strange fire. The *Good News Bible* says they were killed when they offered unholy fire to the Lord. All these translations make it sound as if the sons of Aaron committed some great sin for which they were slain, killed, or put to death by God.

Chaim Ibn Attar, also known as Or HaChayyim, a seventeenth-century popular Orthodox rabbi and highly regarded commentator, had this to say about the deaths of Aaron's sons:

> They approached the supernal light out of their great love of the Holy, and thereby died. Thus, they died by a '*Divine Kiss*,' such as experienced by the perfectly righteous; it is only that the righteous die when the *Divine Kiss* approaches them, while they died by their approaching it. Although they sensed their own demise, this did not prevent them from drawing near to G-d in attachment, delight, delectability, fellowship, love, kissing, and sweetness, to the point that their souls ceased from them.

Why did the sons die? The Bible says they brought strange fire, but if you look at this closely in the original language, it was not the strange fire that caused their death but when they *beqarevatam*. *Beqarevatam* comes from the root word *qarav*, meaning "to come near." The *NIV* and the *ESV* are the closest to the Hebrew, saying they died when they approached or drew near to the Lord. It does not say, as some translations paraphrase, "when they offered or irreverently approached." These interpretations are the translators' own.

Now keep in mind that the tabernacle had just been inaugurated after seven days of waiting for the Divine Presence to make an appearance. This occurred on the eighth day when Aaron offered the first sacrifice and fire came from heaven to light the altar. Eight is the number for the supernatural, the miraculous, and the realm of God. The fire of God came on the eighth day. It was a fire lit by God in a supernatural way. It represented the holiness of God, His passionate love. This was no ordinary fire. This was love itself expressed in a tangible way—the very *racham* love of God coming in the form of fire.

Three thousand years later, that same love would come in the form of a human being called Jesus. It is true that in the natural realm, where time exists, Jesus had not yet come to earth to die on the cross and shed His blood for our sins to bring us the redemption that would purify our souls. But in God's realm, there is no time—past, present, and future coexist. Jesus is the physical manifestation of God, just as the Holy Spirit is often physically manifested as fire, as described in Acts 2:2-4.

The fire of the Holy Spirit is the purifying agent that cleanses the physical body so that the wonders of God may be performed through us. Today, we accept Jesus as our Savior through repentance of our sins, and we are purified to receive the manifestation of the Holy Spirit so we can serve God through His miraculous power and love. In Old Testament times, people were saved the same way—by trusting in a redeemer for their cleansing from sin. Job, who lived a few hundred years before Moses, declared in Job 19:25: "I know my redeemer lives." The word *go'el* (redeemer) is a verb in a participial form, and "lives" is a noun. Thus, in English, we might render this as: "I know my redeemer's life is redeeming." The redemptive work of Jesus was at play from the very beginning of the human race. Even a non-Jew like Job knew there was a redeemer out there who was redeeming him.

It was the priest's duty to keep the fire going so it would never go out. It was also their duty to move the fire from the tabernacle to the temple on Mount Moriah, where Abraham offered his son Isaac as a burnt offering and where Jacob later laid his head and had a vision of a portal to heaven with angels ascending and descending on a ladder. Many Jewish sages believe there is a portal to heaven at this very spot, where the supernatural and natural collide to create a bubble of sorts—the *Tzimtzum*, a space both absent and present. This bubble existed in the Holy of Holies, where a human being could enter the realm of God while still in the physical realm. The problem is that a corruptible human body cannot stand in the presence of an incorruptible God. One's soul needs purification, which only God Himself, through the shed blood of His Son, Jesus Christ, can provide.

Returning to the sons of Aaron, Nadab and Abihu filled an incense burner with "strange fire," and as they approached the Holy of Holies, they were struck dead by the fire of God from heaven. Many interpretations have been offered to explain why the sons of Aaron were struck dead. Early sages suggest that the "strange fire" refers to fire taken from a source other than the sacred fire God sent from heaven. The Hebrew word *zarah* (strange) is the same word used for a prostitute—someone who does not love her client but performs services for a price. The fire sent by

God symbolized His divine *racham* love. In this context, the word "fire" also conveys passionate love. Nadab and Abihu did not take the fire that originated from God's passionate love, thereby profaning the incense. Thus, according to many interpretations, God struck them dead as punishment.

Other less plausible explanations are that the sons were arrogant. They were supposed to be married before they performed their priestly duties. They arrogantly felt that, as the sons of a High Priest, nephews to a king (Moses), and a princess (Miriam), no woman was good enough for them. Some even suggest that as they followed behind their father Aaron and uncle Moses, they thought, "When are these two old men going to die so we can take over?" Of course, that is all speculation because Scripture does not say what their thoughts were or if they were married or not. *Abihu* means "he is a father," which would suggest otherwise, and the name of the other son, *Nadab*, means noble and generous. Arrogance might be far-fetched and grasping at straws to answer this question of why they were struck dead. Some suggested that they wore the wrong garments or that they were not taking their job seriously and just got the fire from another source. Others say it was not laziness but rebellion that caused them to get the strange fire, which is the reason for their deaths. Still, others even speculate this was punishment for Aaron for having agreed to make the golden calf. Another rather far-fetched explanation is that the sons got themselves so drunk that they staggered while carrying the fire, tripped, and the fire caught their robes on fire, burning them to death. However, this does not work because Scripture plainly tells us the fire was sent from heaven.

The only plausible reason was their disobedience in using a strange fire. Yet, if the law was that clear to use the fire from the altar that was set by God, would not Moses and/or Aaron have checked on these two to make sure all was done according to the law? We learn in further verses that Moses was angry with Aaron and his other two sons for eating the goat meat that had been offered as a burnt offering, which Moses believed was forbidden when in mourning. Yet, after Moses sounded off, Aaron calmly explained that only the daily offerings were forbidden to be eaten when in mourning. A special offering, such as this goat offering, was allowed. Moses admitted his error, and all was resolved. It could be that there wasn't a real understanding of the law that required the use of the fire sent from heaven. So, it might have just been a sin of omission rather than a sin of rebellion. But was God that petty? Would He have struck two young priests dead for making a mistake? Perhaps.

But there is another explanation that is popular among rabbis and the sages, and one I feel is the correct reason for the death of Aaron's two sons. Scripture teaches that they carried the burning incense toward the Holy of Holies. Moses said: "I (God) will be sanctified in them that come nigh me, and before all the people I will be glorified." They drew near to the presence of God. Then it says Aaron remained silent when Moses said this was to show that God was holy. Also, there appeared to be no sorrow over this event—no fear descending upon the people. We learn in Leviticus 16:1 that after this event, God warns Aaron not to approach the Holy of Holies anytime he wants but only on a specific occasion.

Note, too, that the sons died by fire from heaven. This heavenly fire has been shown to be an expression of the *racham* love of God. Maybe the sons did not die a violent death but were simply loved to death by God.

The words *come nigh* or *near me* is the word *qarav*, which means not just to draw near but to draw near like a close relative. The view put forth by rabbis in the Talmud and Midrash teaches that these two young men were not arrogant or prideful, nor were they sinful in the ways often suggested. In fact, they were so righteous that, as they approached the Holy of Holies—even sensing their own demise—they continued to draw closer to God in attachment, delight, fellowship, and love, to the point that their souls "ceased from them."

When one receives the *Divine Kiss*, they usually receive it when God draws near to them. But this is a rare case where a natural person had the opportunity to draw close to God. This occurred when the presence of God dwelled in the Holy of Holies over the mercy seat of the Ark of the Covenant.

The reason for the belief that seeing God means death is not that His presence is horrible, like the mask of Medusa, but that when you see the face of God, you will experience the ultimate ecstasy of the soul—the fullness of *racham* love—such that you will not want to return to the work the soul is meant to do within the physical realm. We were sent into this world to impact and transform it, not to escape it. If there was any sin in these two young men, it was allowing themselves to draw too close to God such that their souls desired to leave their bodies and receive the *Divine Kiss*. Moses, Aaron, and Miriam waited for God to approach them with the *Divine Kiss*. The only difference is that *Abihu* and *Nadab* intentionally approached God for the *Divine Kiss*. They died without torment or pain; they passed away in fulfilled joy. But it wasn't yet their time.

Today, there is no temple with a Holy of Holies and an Ark of the Covenant where the Divine Presence rests for us to approach God. We will just have to wait for Him to approach us. When it is our time to leave this body and the physical realm, if we are believers—born again—at that moment, we will experience what unbelievers will not: the ultimate ecstasy of the soul. We will not want to remain in our bodies or even in this realm. We will receive that *Divine Kiss*.

I have heard stories of people saying Jesus appeared to them and spoke with them. Jesus walked into their bedroom and had a chat with them. I will not question the reality of their subjective experience of what they say they saw. But one thing they did not see was His *pani* (presence). If they had seen His presence, they would have experienced what Rabbi Chaim Ibn Attar described as delight, delectability, fellowship, love, kissing, and sweetness, to the point that their souls no longer wanted to exist in their body. Instead, they would have wanted to be permanently attached to the awesome *racham* love of God. Their souls would leave their bodies, and their bodies would cease.

The word we use for a body that ceases is *death*, which is often viewed as something horrible and tragic. Horrible and tragic? Baloney! If Moses had seen the presence of God, or the manifest glory—whatever it was that he hoped to see—God knew his soul would leave his body, and he would not fulfill his mission on earth. In other words, the tragedy of a Christian's death is not that they die but that they fail to fulfill their mission on earth. As Paul said: "For me to live is Christ, to die is gain." (Philippians 1:21).

You can believe what you want, but I stand with Rabbi Chaim Ibn Attar. These men, *Abihu* and *Nadab*, were righteous men who *qarav*, drew near to God, and got such a taste of His *racham* love that they kept moving closer—knowing full well that their physical bodies would cease. But that didn't matter in light of the glory of God that they were beginning to witness. Thus, they received the *Divine Kiss* from God and were welcomed into the presence of God that Moses and his brother Aaron so longed to experience.

8. THE TWO HUNDRED AND FIFTY NASI

And there came out a fire from the LORD, and consumed the two hundred and fifty men that offered incense. (36) And the LORD spake unto Moses, saying, (37) Speak unto Eleazar the son of Aaron the priest, that he take up the censers out of the burning, and scatter thou the fire yonder; for they are hallowed. (40) [To be] a memorial unto the children of Israel, that no stranger, which [is] not of the seed of Aaron, come near to offer incense before the LORD; that he be not as Korah, and as his company: as the LORD said to him by the hand of Moses. (Numbers 16:35-37, 40)

This is an interesting story that hints at the *Divine Kiss*. This story revolves around the incident of Korah, who incited a mutiny challenging Moses' leadership and the granting of the priesthood to Aaron. Korah, a Levite, is accompanied by Dathan and Abiram from the tribe of Reuben, who joined in this coup d'état, as well as 250 *nasi* from various other tribes. The *nasi* were men who were leaders of their community—respected and righteous men. This is where it gets a little tricky.

Korah was of the tribe of Levi but not in the direct line of Aaron. He was a member of the Kehatites, the most prestigious of Levite families. This came down to simply class warfare. Korah wanted to be the high priest, and he promised that if he were to become high priest, he would make everyone equal. That is, he would eliminate the elitism of the priesthood.

Here is the simple question: why would 250 members of the elite of Israel rebel against the elitism of the priesthood? There was no real political power in the priesthood. These 250 men already had all the political power they could want as leaders of their tribes. The priests were merely servants of God, performing the duties of running and maintaining the tabernacle. They had to live off the goodwill offerings of the other eleven tribes. They owned no land and engaged in no commerce as merchants or businessmen. They were not like preachers or evangelists today who maintain a certain amount of political power. If we were to make a comparison, it would not be with the hierarchy and prestige of the clergy, other than those from the house of Aaron. For the most part, the Levites held a position about as enviable as a monk in a monastery, serving as a nun, or even a missionary. No one wants to be a part of that unless they have a burning desire to serve God or draw close to Him. There was really no material or fleshly advantage to being a part of the priesthood.

What the rebels did was really something good. They showed their desire to be close to God by rebelling against the dynastic structure of the priesthood. Korah said it himself and declared that their desire was to be like the priest, whose sole job was to serve God and draw close to Him, but they were forced to live ordinary lives. Numbers 16:3 in the New Living Translation says: *"They united against Moses and Aaron and said, 'You have gone too far! The whole community of Israel has been set apart by the LORD, and He is with all of us.'"* This rebellion wasn't about land rights, food, money, or even political power. It was all about the perceived advantage that the priests had in being able to serve God and draw close to Him. It was an advantage they believed they did not have simply because they were not born into the family of Levi.

They declared that the whole community was set apart by the Lord and that the Lord was with all of them. So why could a person not serve as a priest if they so desired? Why could a Reubenite or a Benjamite not serve as a priest and carry the holy censers if they so wished?

Here is where it gets interesting, and where we can find a present-day application. Although the ground does not crack open and swallow us up, we are guilty of much the same thing today—not jealousy of a position or power structure, but of perceiving that someone in ministry is somehow closer to God than an ordinary janitor or waitress. How many factory workers or service workers run to their priest, pastor, or prophet to be prayed over when they need healing or favor from God, rather than ask a godly father, mother, or grandparent? How many would ask their own brother or sister to pray over them when a godly pastor or priest is available?

Of course, people will choose a pastor or priest over their own mother or father to pray for them, believing that the pastor or priest is closer to God. And if it's a bishop or Area Denominational Supervisor (ADS), that's even better. You can imagine the results if the pope prayed for you. Oh man, that's almost like talking to God Himself—almost a guaranteed answer to prayer! After all, when the pandemic of 2020 was announced, the pope declared to the world he would pray that God would end the pandemic. And guess what? The pandemic eventually ended enough that we could remove our masks. *Praisalleluia* for the pope's prayers! Okay, so it took a couple of years for it to end, but does that suggest the old boy's prayer didn't work?

Things haven't changed much since the days of the Hebrews. Just as we somehow hold this idea that someone who has been to seminary and had hands laid upon them is closer to God than the average person, so too did the Hebrews believe that being born into a Levitical family made one closer to God. Well, Korah and his 250 radicals thought differently. They believed anyone could be close to God and demanded their piece of the priestly pie. "If my little Reuben wants to grow up to be a priest and carry the incense, well, doggone it, he has the right to go to seminary and learn how to carry the incense. Just because his last name isn't Cohen doesn't mean he should be denied that right—umph!"

Well, they had a good point; only they were ahead of their time. That revolution wasn't to take place for another thousand years and would be led by the Messiah, Jesus Christ. 1 Peter 2:9:

> *But ye are a chosen generation, a royal priesthood, an holy nation, a peculiar people; that ye should shew forth the praises of Him who hath called you out of darkness into His marvellous light.*

Today, we have Bible schools and seminaries in every town. Anyone's son or daughter can attend, graduate, and be ordained as a minister of the Gospel. Whether or not they were called by God to that ministry is another matter. Yet, anyone who desires to be a priest unto God can be because we were all made priests by the Messiah, Jesus Christ.

The simple fact is that God is willing to be close to anyone who wants to be close to Him. They didn't have to be a priest. There was nothing more special about a priest in God's eyes than a simple farmer. Both are precious to Him. He created some as farmers and some as priests. God was not playing favorites. We all have a role to play in this world. We all have a mission to accomplish—a purpose for our lives.

The perception that someone who is a priest has special influence with God is a deception from the pits of hell, and that is where the perpetuators of such a perception ended up—literally.

Note what we learn in Numbers 16:8-11:

> *Then Moses spoke again to Korah: "Now listen, you Levites! Does it seem insignificant to you that the God of Israel has chosen you from among all the community of Israel to be near Him so you can serve in the LORD's Tabernacle and stand before the people to minister to them? Korah, He has already given this special ministry to you and your fellow Levites. Are you now demanding the priesthood as well? The LORD is the one you and your followers are really revolting against! For who is Aaron that you are complaining about him?"*

Moses tells these 250 followers of Korach that they already have the privilege of drawing close to God. They were going to get the *Divine Kiss* from God just as the high priest would. There was nothing special in the eyes of God about being a priest. No special spiritual perks. But they still wanted to be priests to stand before the people and perform priestly functions. Now Moses is addressing the factors of pride, power, and influence. He is getting to the heart of the issue. Is it really about drawing close to God that they want? Or is it about having a sense of being spiritually superior to others? We assume that the 250 rejected this notion and refused to admit to their pride. But how do we know that for sure? Scripture is not clear if they examined their motives or not. It is possible they still longed to be close to God despite having ulterior motives.

I have met many pastors who were truly Godly men. I could sense the presence of God in their lives and the power of God, yet I could not help but feel that sense of entitlement because they had "Rev." before their name. I remember one pastor I knew when I was a young pastor myself, someone I would go to for counsel. My kid brother eventually worked for this pastor as his assistant, and my brother used to say, "When people pray, God listens, but when Pastor A prays, God smiles." Yet, I also sensed pride in this pastor. He was ambitious and eventually drove his church into bankruptcy with his schemes of building a megachurch. People literally worshipped this man and would go to him before anyone else to be prayed over, feeling he had some special connection to God. I never heard him deny such a thing. I honestly believed he felt he had the ear of God more than anyone in his congregation. Yet, he truly loved God with all his heart, I believe that. But he was also human, and there was no one who could reel him in when he felt he was commissioned by God.

I believe God was using him despite this human tendency to take himself and his position as a pastor too seriously. Yet, time eventually proved he was following his own plan and not God's. His great plans to build a conference center and Christian college with a television network never left the ground, and what little he was able to build went into bankruptcy before they even had a chance to hold their first conference. God took him home a year later. I believe with all my heart he met Jesus with that *Divine Kiss*. If I didn't believe that, there would be little hope for me.

I believe Pastor A was truly a man of God, a man with prophetic gifts. He was also a human with human flaws like all of us. Whatever God's plan was for Pastor A, it was fulfilled, and Pastor A is now home in the heart of the God he dearly loved. The people of Israel did not realize that a special position of priesthood also came with special responsibilities. When you are on the front lines, you will receive the most fire from the enemy and need the prayer support of those who are not on the front lines. I recently read that in World War II, only one in every sixteen soldiers in uniform ever saw combat. That meant less than 15% of those in uniform had glorious stories to tell of heroics under fire. The other 85% spent their time repairing airplanes and tanks, shipping goods to the front line, building bases, working logistics, and performing all the other support those on the front lines needed to perform their heroics. Those 85% may not have had glorious stories to tell, but they did their job. They saluted their flag, faced fire if necessary, and deserve the same honor as anyone who wore the uniform and was honorably discharged when the time came.

The issue before the 250 was simply that they wanted to serve on the front lines. They wanted some of that glory, even though they already wore the "uniform" of the chosen of God.

When judgment time came and God revealed who were His chosen front-line warriors for the specific task of priesthood and spiritual leadership—and who were not—those who were not ended up swallowed by an earthquake. Numbers 16:30-35 records:

> *But if the LORD does something entirely new and the ground opens its mouth and swallows them and all their belongings, and they go down alive into the grave, then you will know that these men have shown contempt for the LORD.*

He had hardly finished speaking the words when the ground suddenly split open beneath them. The earth opened its mouth and swallowed the men, along with their households and all their followers who were standing with them, and everything they owned. So they went down alive into the grave, along with all their belongings. The earth closed over them, and they all vanished from among the people of Israel. All the people around them fled when they heard their screams. "The earth will swallow us, too!" they cried. Then fire blazed forth from the LORD and burned up the 250 men who were offering incense.

The 250 *nasi*—the elite of every tribe, the men of renown—were not swallowed by the earthquake. They were consumed by the fire of God, the fire of His *racham*, His passionate love. Moses said nothing about those consumed by the fire as having shown contempt for the Lord; only those swallowed by the earth were said to show contempt. Why were the men who offered incense not swallowed by the earth? Perhaps it was because they did not show contempt for the Lord.

The word "contempt" is *na'ats* in Hebrew. It is really a word for rejection. Korach and his followers, who were swallowed by the earthquake, rejected the Lord. The 250 did not reject the Lord; they rejected Moses' message that they were already fulfilling the roles they wanted. Perhaps they sincerely wanted to be close to God and felt that the elitism of the priesthood stood in their way. After all, they came with their incense offerings.

Now, that is the crux of the matter—the censers with the incense offerings. This was what the sons of Aaron carried to the Holy of Holies when they were struck down by the fire of God. It is almost a footnote in verse 35 that the 250 were consumed by fire. As I previously discussed, the sons of Aaron who offered strange fire were struck down by God's fire. I believe this is the same situation with these 250 *nasi*. Like the sons of Aaron, they wanted to touch the face of God. Scripture tells us they were near the tabernacle. They likely did not light their incense with the fire from heaven but brought strange fire, like the sons of Aaron, before the Holy of Holies. If they used the fire from the altar, they still were not consecrated to approach the Holy of Holies. When they continued to approach the Holy of Holies with strange fire, they were drawn into the presence of God, like the sons of Aaron, who were in disobedience but longed to be near God. Like the sons of Aaron, I believe they received what the Talmud teaches was the *Divine Kiss* and were brought into the presence of God.

The fire, as a symbol of the Divine Passionate Love of God, may have consumed their bodies, but they were drawn into the presence of God. Their demise was not the result of rebellion like the followers of Korach. Their demise was the *Divine Kiss*; they saw the "Face of God," and their spirits could not remain in their bodies. Their spirits had to leave their bodies to be joined with their Creator. We say they "died." That word "died" is very misleading. Their bodies ceased, but they did not cease to exist—they did not die.

You see, a Christian will never die. That is, if you use the word "death" only in the context of separation from God. We will never be separated from God. We will be separated from this corrupt, sinful body, but that is not death. It is for the unbeliever to die, for death separates the unbeliever from the only possible link to God, and thus they do die spiritually.

Here's my idea. I suppose most won't like it, but I believe these 250 men did not reject God. They simply committed an act of disobedience in their desire to be close to God in a way that was forbidden in this lifetime, and they were raptured. Yes, I believe all believers are raptured. Okay, not quite like being taken to heaven in a physical body, but who wants to spend eternity in this broken-down shell? How about we just get raptured out of this old shell and into the presence of God?

Oh, you say, these 250 *nasi* were in disobedience. How could they experience such an honorable ending to this physical life? Well, pray tell, how many believers will be in disobedience when the rapture occurs? We are not perfect and will never be perfect while in this flesh.

People call the rapture the blessed hope. Indeed, it is the blessed hope, but not just this rapture before a seven-year tribulation. What is the difference between getting raptured in this old corrupt body and being presented to God in a new body, rather than just leaving this shell on earth and appearing before God in a new body? In my thinking, it is just one and the same. Appearing before God in the body or out of the body? Even the Apostle Paul did not know the difference. As he wrote in 2 Corinthians 12:3: *"And I know that this man—whether in the body or apart from the body I do not know, but God knows."*

Paul paid a visit to paradise, and he did not even know if he was in the body or out of the body. Can you dig it? You wouldn't even know if you had left your body or not. So, what difference does it make if you are raptured before the tribulation or you pass from this world through natural causes and your spirit leaves your body to be joined with a new one? Same thing, is it not? Why is this rapture business such a big deal? We will all get raptured. In the long run, we won't even know the difference.

9. UZZAH AND THE ARK

And he smote the men of Bethshemesh, because they had looked into the ark of the LORD, even he smote of the people fifty thousand and threescore and ten men: and the people lamented, because the LORD had smitten many of the people with a great slaughter. (I Samuel 6:19)

"And the anger of the LORD was kindled against Uzza, and he smote him, because he put his hand to the ark: and there he died before God." (I Chronicles 13:10)

There are many miracles associated with the ark. As mentioned in the previous chapter, the ark was a "ghost ark"—present but absent at the same time. Another strange characteristic of the ark, according to the Midrash in *Yalkut Shimoni Shmuel II 5:142*, is the belief by many mystical Jews that the ark actually carried its carriers. When the priests lifted the ark for transport, instead of carrying the ark, the ark carried them. The poles used by the priests to lift the ark were never to be removed. Only a specific sect of priests were permitted to carry the ark. In Numbers 7:9, we learn that the family of Kehat was assigned the duty of carrying the ark and was specifically instructed to *"carry it on their shoulders."* The ark was to move on its own accord, not to be transported on a wagon, especially one being pulled or powered by natural forces. Its movement was to be purely supernatural.

In I Samuel 4-6, we read about the Philistines defeating the Israelites and capturing the ark. However, plagues and afflictions fell upon the Philistines due to their possession of the ark. It even destroyed their idol Dagon when placed in Dagon's temple. The Philistines finally returned the ark to Israel in a cart, after which the Levites immediately removed the ark and used the cart's wood to offer a sacrifice with the cows that had pulled it.

We further read in I Samuel 6:19:

> *And he smote the men of Bethshemesh, because they had looked into the ark of the LORD, even he smote of the people fifty thousand and threescore and ten men: and the people lamented, because the LORD had smitten many of the people with a great slaughter.*

The specifics of how these 50,070 people died are disputed because the Hebrew text is unclear. The numerical phrasing deviates from the normal order, and the absence of a conjunction between "seventy men" and "50,000 men" suggests that Josephus may be correct in asserting that some Hebrew manuscripts omitted the 50,000 entirely. This is particularly plausible since the village of Beth-shemesh could not have contained such a large population. Others argue that 70 represents the number of those who died, while 50,000 refers to the number of those present. In other words, only 70 came close enough to the Ark to be slain.

Regardless of the exact number, many people died after the Ark was opened. Various explanations have been proposed, ranging from disrespect toward the Ark to disobedience of God's laws. Some suggest that they were not properly sanctified or purified before drawing close to inspect the Ark's contents. I would align with the latter explanation, adding that their deaths occurred because they entered into the *tzim tzum*—the bubble between heaven and earth—where only a sinless, properly cleansed physical body could survive. Otherwise, their corruptible bodies could not exist in that realm.

God operates in two opposite modes: the revealed or natural realm and the concealed or supernatural realm. In the natural realm, there is an apparent lack of Divinity, stemming from God's ability to conceal Himself. Miracles, which break the laws of the natural world, represent openings into God's concealed realm. However, God transcends both the natural and supernatural realms. He is neither entirely concealed nor entirely revealed but exists beyond both and can unite the two modalities at will.

Humankind, being limited to the natural realm, cannot pass into the supernatural realm in a physical body. Any attempt to do so without the covering of Jesus' blood results in the destruction of the human body.

The Ark was placed in the Holy of Holies, the most sacred spot on earth, where God's supernatural reality was revealed. Thus, the Ark occupied space in the natural realm while simultaneously existing in the supernatural realm. As sages have said, it was the perfect kiss between heaven and earth.

When a believer approaches death, they too, through God's grace and power, occupy both realms simultaneously. This was exemplified on the Mount of Transfiguration, where Peter, James, and John (from the natural realm) were joined by Moses and Elijah (from the supernatural realm). Similarly, when we pass from this world, God will invite us into the *tzim tzum*—that bubble containing both heaven and earth—where we will receive the *Divine Kiss*. Like Peter on the Mount of Transfiguration, we may want to dwell there, but unlike Peter, our mission will have been completed, and we will enter the Father's house.

When the priests were returning the Ark to its permanent place after its captivity by the Philistines, they disobeyed Hebraic law. They placed the Ark on a cart pulled by oxen, completely disregarding God's commands. If they neglected this law, it is likely they also neglected the purification procedures required of priests handling the Ark.

When it appeared that the Ark might fall off the cart, Uzzah reached out to steady it, treating it as if it were ordinary furniture. However, by doing so, he entered the *tzim tzum,* and his body was instantly destroyed. Unlike Nadab, Abihu, and the 250 *nasi*, Uzzah was not prepared to enter the *tzim tzum,* nor was he seeking to draw closer to God. To him, the Ark was merely another object, and he failed to respect its sacred significance.

10. THE MARRIAGE PICTURE

"When as His mother Mary was espoused to Joseph, before they came together, she was found with child of the Holy Spirit." (Matthew 1:18)

In the time that Jesus was born, arranged marriages were customary. This practice had practical reasons, as travel and communication were still quite primitive, and communities had limited contact with each other. Finding a suitable mate was often challenging, as potential marriage partners within a community were scarce. There wasn't always a "girl next door" available for marriage. Thus, the role of a matchmaker became essential. Matchmakers traveled to various towns to find suitable matches for young men and women of marriageable age. It was not unusual for a young couple to meet for the first time on their wedding day.

Take, for example, Abraham, who could not find a proper match for Isaac within his community and had to send his servant on a 400-mile journey to find a suitable bride. The arrangements and marriage contracts were made before Isaac and Rebecca even met. Due to the distance, a pre-wedding meeting was impractical. Until modern transportation and communication evolved, many young couples likely held hands and kissed for the first time during the wedding ceremony.

Marriage was not based on love or compatibility. Couples simply followed their parents' orders and traditions, trusting that they would eventually "learn to love" each other. While meaningful intimacy is enhanced when love exists between a couple, in many cases, love developed gradually over time. Jennette Oke's *Love Comes Softly* describes this perfectly—a couple marries out of convenience and, over time, realizes they truly love one another.

In some cases, love happened at first sight. The Bible tells us that Isaac loved Rebecca the moment he first saw her. However, most people desired some history or foundation before entering physical intimacy. To address this, the tradition of betrothal was developed.

During a betrothal, a couple was officially married. They signed a *ketubah* (marriage contract) and paid a dowry. However, there was no wedding celebration, and the couple was immediately separated. The bride continued living with her parents or, if living far away, in a tent or separate accommodations. The bride and groom would live apart for at least a year.

During this time, the groom was not expected to work but was supported by his parents. He spent the year doing two things: building an additional room onto his father's house for him and his bride and getting to know his new wife. The couple shared romantic walks, discussed their future, shared their dreams and fears, and grew emotionally and intellectually intimate—but not physically.

After a year, the groom, filled with desire and anticipation, would finally sneak to his bride's house to take her to his father's home. The bridal party, having kept oil in their lamps for this moment, would light the lamps and join the procession, following the groom to his bride's house. The groom would then carry his bride (hence the custom of carrying the bride over the threshold) to his father's house, where a grand celebration lasting at least three days would take place. The couple would consummate their marriage in the *yichud* room or tent while the guests partied.

Though variations exist, this was the general custom. It was not much different from modern engagements, except that a betrothal legally bound the couple. Breaking a betrothal required a formal divorce.

The story of Mary and Joseph introduces an interesting twist. Joseph had grounds to end his betrothal to Mary when it was discovered she was pregnant. This would have been a scandal, as betrothal laws forbade physical intimacy before the betrothal period ended. Joseph could have been accused of adultery if he stayed with Mary.

What does all this have to do with the *Divine Kiss* or death? A beautiful parallel exists between the institution of marriage and our spiritual relationship with God. Our earthly life is akin to the betrothal period. We are spiritually married to God but have not yet consummated the relationship. The consummation occurs when we leave this physical body and enter the Father's house, symbolizing eternal unity with God.

Matthew 1:18 sets the stage for this understanding. Mary, the mother of Jesus, was betrothed to Joseph. Joseph was described as a just man, and cultural context suggests he was likely older than Mary, possibly a widower. Mary, still a virgin, would have been around 14 years old, as puberty marked the age of marriage readiness, even as young as 10 or 11.

Under Jewish tradition, betrothal equaled legal marriage, yet the couple could not live together or have physical intimacy for at least a year. This period allowed the couple to develop emotional intimacy. However, for someone entering a second marriage, this waiting period was not always required.

This seems to be the case with Mary and Joseph. An older man who was a widower would not be required to go through a year-long betrothal. A couple of weeks, or no waiting period at all, might be required for an older, previously married man.

To avoid scandal when Mary's pregnancy was revealed to Joseph, and after receiving assurance from the angel, Joseph decided to take Mary into his home immediately. Typically, first-century Jewish women would not reveal a pregnancy until about five months along. Following this tradition, Joseph's decision to bring Mary into his home early would lead others to assume that Joseph was the father when the pregnancy became apparent.

For someone who had a prior marriage, as was likely the case with Joseph, he could terminate the betrothal anytime and consummate the marriage without much controversy.

The primary purpose of betrothal was to allow a couple to spend quality time together and develop a loving relationship. Another important purpose was to give the bridegroom time to build an addition to his father's house. The imagery of the bridegroom preparing a place for his bride in his father's house resonates with John 14:2-3:

> *In my Father's house are many mansions: if it were not so, I would have told you. I go to prepare a place for you. And if I go and prepare a place for you, I will come again, and receive you unto myself; that where I am, there ye may be also.*

Here, Jesus illustrates that our relationship with Him is like a betrothal period that takes place while we live on earth. During this time, we grow deeply in love with Him. We are legally married to Jesus when we accept Him as our personal Savior, but the marriage is not consummated until He returns to take us to His Father's house. Our time on earth is meant to know Him more—through His Word and through our daily walk with Him. One day, He will return to consummate the marriage in His Father's house, which we call heaven.

The year-long betrothal period forbade physical intimacy between the bride and bridegroom. This period created such longing and desire that, when the time finally came, the consummation of the marriage became all the more fulfilling.

This idea ties to the Jewish teaching of the *Divine Kiss*. When the betrothal period ended, and the bridegroom was finally alone with his bride after a year of anticipation, he would give her a deep, loving, and satisfying kiss as they entered the *yichud* room as husband and wife.

This is a picture of our relationship with Jesus, who is preparing a room for us in His Father's house. During this betrothal, He is with us every moment, allowing us to grow closer to Him. The more we experience life with Him, the more we long to be united with Him as one, to receive that *Divine Kiss*, and to finally rest in His Father's house.

For the believer, death is not a horrible, tragic experience—it is our Divine hope. It is a personal rapture without the Second Coming. It is the moment when we leave the world we have known and enter the presence of our beloved Bridegroom, into the place He has prepared for us.

The bridegroom spent an entire year preparing a place for his bride in his father's house. This home would be part of a larger structure—a palace or castle—housing an entire family, including brothers, sisters, their spouses, and children. Each family member had a private apartment prepared by the bridegroom, designed to suit the bride's tastes and desires.

To illustrate, I recall an elderly woman whose grown children wanted her to sell her home after her husband of many years had passed. They encouraged her to move into a senior living apartment complex closer to them, with medical staff and maintenance support. However, she refused to leave her home.

With tears in her eyes, she pointed to a built-in bookcase and explained how her late husband, a skilled carpenter, had built it for her because of her love for books. She went on to describe every detail of their home— the kitchen cabinets built as an anniversary gift, the remodeled bathroom crafted as a birthday present. Every corner of the house reflected her husband's love and care for her.

In tears, she said, "My husband is gone, but every morning, I wake up and see and hear my husband saying, 'I love you' in this house he prepared just for me. Every cabinet, every wall cries out, 'I love you.'"

Similarly, we are in a period of betrothal, during which we are learning to love our Bridegroom, Jesus Christ. One day, this period will end, and He will snatch us away to His Father's house. There, we will dwell in a place designed and prepared just for us, with every detail proclaiming, "I love you."

11. THE DIVINE HUG

"My soul follows hard after you; your right hand upholds me." (Psalm 63:8)

If our sojourn here on earth is a betrothal period and we are awaiting that *Divine Kiss* where Jesus takes us to His Father's house, wouldn't He give us a little taste of what to expect? I believe within Jewish teaching there is a hint of something that God does to give us a glimpse of our eternal state—our consummation of marriage with Him. I call it a *Divine Hug.* The Jews call it a *devequt.*

In my reading of various Jewish works, I found records of rabbis entering a state of *devequt* during prayer. As I continue my journey to discover the heart of God, I am increasingly fascinated by the Jewish sages' devotion to prayer as a means of achieving oneness with God. There is a record of one rabbi who would roll on the floor while praying, crying out, "I don't want to enter the Garden of Eden, I don't want to enter the Kingdom of God, I just want God." Another account tells of a rabbi who entered such a deep state of prayer that he asked God to let him remain with Him forever. On one occasion, this rabbi's family was frightened as they saw him in such a deep state of *devequt.* When his son tried to shake him out of his prayer, the rabbi collapsed into his son's arms and passed away. There are multiple accounts of rabbis who died while in a state of *devequt,* experiencing what they described as a *Divine Kiss* during this moment of deep communion.

Now, I am not advocating for such extreme devotion to prayer. However, this concept of *devequt* makes me wonder if my personal prayer life has barely scratched the surface of what is possible. My study of the word *devequt* is what inspired this book on the *Divine Kiss*.

We first encounter the word *devequt* in Genesis 2:24: *"Therefore shall a man leave his father and his mother, and shall cleave unto his wife: and they shall be one flesh."*

The word *cleave* or *cling* is *devequt*. In Hebrew, *devequt* means overtaking, reaching, or clinging. Jewish teachers describe *devequt* as a practice of adherence to or communion with God, often likened to a mystical union with Him. Mysticism is sometimes a misunderstood concept among Christians. When we hear the term, we may think of magicians or those performing supernatural acts. However, Jewish mysticism, as I understand it, involves a deep, personal relationship with God. It is the belief that one can pray to God, feel His presence, and experience His love. By this definition, many Christians, including myself, would be considered mystics.

Thus, *devequt*—a mystical union with God—is simply entering a deep love relationship with Him where one experiences His divine presence. This notion stems from the Biblical command to love the Lord with all your heart, soul, and might, to walk in His ways, and to hold fast to Him. Some describe *devequt* as entering a meditative, trance-like state during prayer. However, my study of this practice reveals that it does not necessarily involve an actual trance.

In modern Christian context, this may resemble what is called "soaking," which emerged during the Toronto Blessing. Many years ago, my brother took me to the Toronto Airport Vineyard Church, where I witnessed people lying on the floor, often silent, simply enjoying the presence of God. They called this "soaking." It was not about offering prayers or requests but simply being in God's presence—similar to lovers quietly enjoying each other's company. A Jewish rabbi might call this *devequt*.

Some have criticized soaking, claiming it opens one to demonic activity. However, as I studied *devequt*, I found Scriptural support for this practice, particularly in Psalms 63:8: *"My soul follows hard after you; your right hand upholds me."*

The phrase "follows hard" is the Hebrew *devequt*, which some translations render as "clings." I think of it as practicing hugging God and allowing Him to hug you. Many who soak describe imagining God hugging them while they express love, praise, and worship. God exists outside of time, so He has all the time in the world to lavish His love upon us. The question is, how much time are we willing to invest in letting Him do so?

When I feel troubled, I often turn to the Psalms, particularly Psalm 63. I am drawn to verse 8, where David speaks of following hard after God or clinging to Him: *"Deveqah nepeshi acherika" (My soul clings to You).*

Jewish sages teach that *devequt* is a gateway to God's heart through holiness and sanctification. This suggests that King David himself practiced what we might now call soaking or *devequt*. For David, this was likely not a specific practice but a natural way of life, much like how lovers hold hands, hug, or kiss as a normal part of their relationship.

In Psalm 63, David's hunger for God leads him into a state of *devequt*—a spiritual clinging or hugging of God. One Jewish writer describes this type of prayer as seeking nothing for oneself but seeking to bring pleasure to God, a state of total humility. The Hebrew word for humility, *anavah*, does not mean thinking little of oneself. Rather, it means losing all sense of self in the presence of God. It is in this state of humility that one enters *devequt*.

Some evangelical Christians may frown upon such practices. In my Baptist tradition, I was taught that deep meditative states in prayer could be dangerous, potentially allowing the devil to take advantage. But such fears seem misplaced when we consider the context of *devequt*.

Letting go of ourselves in the presence of God is not a moment of vulnerability to evil; it is an opportunity to experience His overwhelming love and presence. To me, *devequt*—whether called soaking, clinging, or simply being still in God's presence—is a practice that draws us closer to the Divine.

We find in C.S. Lewis's book series *The Chronicles of Narnia,* in the final book of the series entitled *The Last Battle,* a scene where a warrior who had fought for Tash—the Satanic figure—suddenly finds himself confronted with Aslan, the Christ figure. Realizing that he had been serving the wrong master all his life, the warrior laments his actions. Aslan bends down and reassures him that he is welcomed into His kingdom, explaining that Tash and Aslan are opposites. Aslan says:

> I take to me the services which thou hast done to him. For I and he are of such different kinds that no service which is vile can be done to me, and none which is not vile can be done to him.

In other words, if you are soaking or practicing *devequt* with a pure heart—a heart filled with love and a desire to draw close to God—the enemy cannot infiltrate that sacred space. However, if you engage in these practices with a selfish heart, hoping to bribe God into granting blessings or power, you may indeed open yourself to something that is the opposite of God.

Returning to the analogy of a man and wife on their honeymoon, imagine an old girlfriend entering the room, saying, "I will take over." Such a thing would not happen unless the man desires the old girlfriend more than his wife, which is highly unlikely. Similarly, David says in the Psalms that the *"right hand of God sustains me."* The right hand of God represents His power. David is saying that even if he enters a state of *devequt* with motives that are not entirely pure, he trusts that the power of God will protect him from any evil trying to disrupt this intimate relationship.

Here's the clincher: you don't need to enter a trance-like state to experience *devequt*. *Devequt* is simply about losing all sense of self. There's an old saying: "Looking out for number one." In this case, number one is *Aleph*, or God. A state of *devequt* is seeking only one thing: to please the God you love.

Helen Lemmel wrote a hymn back in 1922. She had been married to a wealthy man, but at the age of fifty-five, she went completely blind. Her husband abandoned her, leaving her with nothing. Destitute and heartbroken, Helen turned her unseeing eyes to Jesus. In her darkest hour, she wrote a hymn that became beloved around the world:

"Turn your eyes upon Jesus,
Look full in His wonderful face,
And the things of earth will grow strangely dim,
In the light of His glory and grace."

I firmly believe that Helen entered a state of *devequt.* She approached Jesus not to ask for her sight, not to plead for relief from heartbreak, nor to seek deliverance from poverty. She came to simply please Him with what little she had. In return, God gave her a *Divine Hug* that sustained her for the next forty-three years, until one day, He gave her a *Divine Kiss* and welcomed her to His Father's house.

We all have needs and desires, and it is natural for our prayers to be filled with requests for God to meet those needs. Scripture encourages us to make our requests known to the Lord. However, Scripture also speaks about *devequt*—a state of prayer where we ask for nothing and seek only to draw closer to God.

Jeremiah 29:13 tells us, *"You will seek me and find me when you seek me with all your heart."*

The *Divine Hug* comes when we seek and search for God with all our hearts—confessing our sins, repenting, and waiting upon the Lord.

Perhaps now is the time to begin your quest to discover the heart of God by seeking and receiving His *devequt,* His *Divine Hug.*

12. TASTE DEATH

"Verily I say unto you, There be some standing here, which shall not taste of death, till they see the Son of man coming in his kingdom." (Matthew 16:28)

Reading this at face value can be quite confusing. At first glance, it appears to refer to the Second Coming of Jesus, yet it says that some of those present with Jesus would not die before His return. However, the text specifically says they would not "taste death." Isn't that the same as dying?

Commentators have wrestled with this passage and often conclude that Jesus was referring to certain aspects of the Kingdom of God, such as the resurrection, the transfiguration, or the ascension into heaven. While these explanations attempt to protect the integrity of God's Word, they fail to capture the full context. Jesus didn't say they would see only a portion of the kingdom; He explicitly stated that they would see the entire kingdom.

Others interpret the "taste of death" as a first-century idiom referring to one's legacy. This explanation could hold merit, as the disciples' memory and legacy remain alive 2,000 years later and will continue until Jesus returns. However, this interpretation implies that their legacy would end when Jesus establishes His kingdom, which raises questions. It seems reasonable that, once Jesus returns, the disciples' mission will reach ful-fillment, making their earthly legacy no longer necessary.

Let's take a closer look at the phrase *taste of death.* In Greek, the words are *geusontai thanatou. Geusontai* means "to taste, experience, or partake," and *thanatou* refers to the separation of the soul from the body, encom-passing either spiritual or physical death. This passage cannot refer to spiritual death, as it pertains to the disciples, who were assured of eternal life. Thus, it must be referencing physical death.

Jesus likely spoke these words in Aramaic, which sheds additional light on this passage. The Aramaic word for "taste" is *taim,* which I discovered in Jewish literature, including the Targum, to have a nuanced meaning. In first-century Jewish understanding, *taim* was used to express the value of what was consumed. For instance, certain foods were deemed healthi-er than others. In the Book of Daniel, we read that Daniel and his friends chose kosher food, and their attendant, concerned for their appearance, soon discovered the *taim*—the value—of the kosher diet.

Thus, Jesus could be saying: *"Verily I say unto you, There be some standing here, those who shall not see the value of death, till they see the Son of man coming in his kingdom."*

Indeed, the disciples, at the time of their death, may not have fully un-derstood the value of the coming Kingdom of God. However, once they entered eternity—where time ceases to exist—everything became clear. As 2 Peter 3:8 reminds us, *"One day with the Lord is as a thousand years."* After stepping into heaven, they would see the immense value of the Son of Man coming in His kingdom.

In life, the disciples willingly gave up everything, even their lives, for the sake of Jesus and the Gospel. However, it was not until after death that they would fully comprehend the eternal value of their sacrifice.

For many of us, death is something we fear. Yet, when we surrender our lives for Jesus, we willingly go beyond that fear. Only after passing into the Kingdom of God do we realize how unnecessary our fear of death was. Death is not the end; it is the doorway to something far greater. Some will not "taste"—*taim,* or value—death until they see the Son of Man coming in His kingdom.

The Talmud teaches that a man can describe the taste of meat to someone who has never eaten it, using every conceivable word. Yet, only after tasting it for themselves will they truly understand its flavor. Similarly, the martyrs throughout history had an idea of what they were dying for, but it was only after death that they fully grasped the value of their sacrifice.

The word for death, *mutha,* like its Greek counterpart, can mean either spiritual or physical death. Another interpretation is that the Kingdom of God belongs to those who accept Jesus as their Savior. Until we die to ourselves—our fleshly, selfish, earthly desires—and embrace the spiritual life Jesus offers, we cannot see the *taim,* the true value, of the Son of Man coming in His Kingdom.

Some Biblical scholars argue that *"seeing the Son of Man coming in His Kingdom"* refers to the Transfiguration. This event, though mysterious to many Christians, finds possible explanations within Jewish teachings, offering a glimpse of Jesus' divine glory.

13. TZIM TZUM AND THE TRANSFIGURATION

Thou shalt bring them in, and plant them in the mountain of thine inheritance, in the place, O LORD, which thou hast made for thee to dwell in, in the Sanctuary, O Lord, which thy hands have established. The LORD shall reign for ever and ever. (Exodus 15:17-18)

I knew a man in Christ above fourteen years ago, (whether in the body, I cannot tell; or whether out of the body, I cannot tell: God knoweth;) such an one caught up to the third heaven. And I know such a man--whether in the body or out of the body, I do not know; God knows. How that he was caught up into paradise, and heard unspeakable words, which it is not lawful for a man to utter. (II Corinthians 12:2-4)

"And the temple of God was opened in heaven, and there was seen in his temple the ark of his testament." (Revelation 11:19)

And after six days Jesus taketh Peter, James, and John his brother, and bringeth them up into an high mountain apart, And was transfigured before them: and his face did shine as the sun, and his raiment was white as the light. And, behold, there appeared unto them Moses and Elias talking with him. (Matthew 17:1-3)

It seems that moments—perhaps hours, days, weeks, or even months—before someone passes, God begins the process of a *Divine Kiss*, which

I call a *Divine Hug*. The Jews refer to this as entering a state of *devequt*. Does one enter another realm in a state of *devequt*? Is there a state between heaven and earth, as found in many belief systems, where a soul temporarily resides? I believe the story of the Transfiguration offers us a clue. Here, we have an example of interaction between human beings—Peter, James, and John—who were still in physical bodies on earth, and those who had been taken to heaven, namely Moses and Elijah.

Whether Moses and Elijah were still in corrupt physical bodies is debatable. One thing is certain: unless their corrupt bodies were transformed into glorified bodies, like that of Jesus, they could not have survived in outer space or however the journey to heaven occurs. Their bodies had to be glorified to preserve their physical organs from dying. This concept will be explored further in a later chapter.

Another debated issue arises from the Gospels of Matthew, Mark, and Luke, where Jesus told His disciples that some of them would not taste death until they saw the coming of the Son of Man in His Kingdom. If this referred to the Second Coming, how could all the disciples have died before the event occurred, as it has not yet happened? Many scholars believe this prophecy was fulfilled on the Mount of Transfiguration. If this is the case, how could Peter, James, and John have witnessed this event, seemingly beyond space and time, while still in corruptible physical bodies that had not yet tasted death but survived outside the natural realm?

This aspect of the Transfiguration has always been a mystery to me until I encountered the Jewish concept of *tzim tzum*, which literally means "reduction" and is a paradox of presence in absence. To understand *tzim tzum*, we need to revisit the Old Testament and the story of the Ark of the Covenant.

Years ago, while working for Dr. Lester Sumrall's ministry, someone asked him about the location of the Ark of the Covenant. Rather than referring to speculative theories, he cited Revelation 11:19, which states that the temple of God in heaven contains the Ark of the Testament, another term for the Ark of the Covenant. Thus, Dr. Sumrall concluded that the Ark is in heaven.

Initially, I thought this was an overly simplistic explanation. However, after years of studying Jewish works, I am inclined to agree. Jewish Orthodox teaching describes the Ark of the Covenant as a "ghost covenant." According to the Talmud (*Yoma* 21a, *Megillah* 10b, and *Bava Batra* 99a), the Ark did not occupy space. The Holy of Holies, where the Ark resided, measured ten cubits wide, yet the Ark, which was 2.5 cubits long, stood in the center. Measurements from the sides of the Ark to the walls still totaled five cubits on each side. The Ark simultaneously occupied space and did not—a mystery that aligns with the concept of *tzim tzum.*

When the presence of God rested upon the Ark, it existed both in heaven and on earth at the same time. This phenomenon, called *tzim tzum,* means the Ark was present but not present. In other words, the Ark, bearing God's presence, was not entirely in this physical realm, yet it was. This concept is as mysterious as the Trinity, defying explanation.

Quantum physics brings us closer to understanding *tzim tzum* with theories of alternative or parallel universes. Some stories, though unproven, suggest individuals have briefly entered these parallel realms. For example, a woman might wake up to find she works in a different office or job, only to return to her original reality the next day. Science fiction often explores such ideas, as in the series *Sliders,* where a young physicist creates a wormhole leading to alternate worlds. These parallel dimensions offer a glimpse of *tzim tzum.*

The Third Heaven, as mentioned in II Corinthians 12:2-4, may be an example of *tzim tzum.* The Apostle Paul describes being caught up to the Third Heaven and then to paradise. Some interpret these as the same place, but the text could imply two separate locations. It's plausible to speculate that the Third Heaven houses the Third Temple.

Revelation 11:19 states that the temple in heaven contains the Ark of the Covenant. Could this Third Heaven be an alternate universe where the Ark resides and where God's presence intersects with our natural realm? Dispensationalists often interpret this as a mere vision, but who's to say a vision isn't a portal into another universe, what Paul calls the Third Heaven?

Paul had been a member of the Sanhedrin and a Pharisee. He was a Jew among Jews, deeply immersed in Jewish traditions and teachings. The temple would have had great sentimental value to him, and he knew that the Second Temple would be destroyed—not only from the teachings of

Jesus but also from the realization that the Second Temple was not built according to the exact design of God and therefore had to be destroyed. Hence, God taking him to the dimension or alternative universe where the Third Temple exists and was built by Messiah Jesus would have been a great comfort to him.

If the Third Temple is already in heaven with the Ark of the Covenant, how do you explain II Thessalonians 2:4? *"Who opposeth and exalteth himself above all that is called God, or that is worshipped; so that he as God sitteth in the temple of God, shewing himself that he is God."*

According to the popular dispensationalist view, the appearance of the antichrist corresponds with the events of the Book of Revelation, as interpreted by figures like Hal Lindsey and the *Left Behind* series, among others. These events are seen as future occurrences, requiring a temple in Israel yet to be built. After all, if the antichrist is to appear, he needs a temple in which to sit. So, how can the Third Temple be on earth and in heaven simultaneously?

I am not a dispensationalist or pre-millennialist, but I can see possible explanations. One possibility involves *tzim tzum.* However, according to II Thessalonians, the antichrist will set himself up as God, sitting in the temple. This would mean the antichrist would actually enter the Holy of Holies and sit on the Ark of the Covenant—a scenario that seems highly unlikely.

Another possibility is that a temple will be built, but it will not be the true Third Temple. The Ark of the Covenant might be either discovered or remanufactured. If discovered, it is likely not the original Ark but a replica unearthed in an archaeological dig and declared authentic by so-called experts—or a counterfeit Ark could be fabricated and declared real. This would allow for the construction of a "temple" capable of seating the antichrist. Such a deception would require a grand-scale conspiracy, yet it is conceivable, especially given the supernatural powers attributed to the antichrist.

This theory might explain why Paul refers to his visit as a trip to the Third Heaven rather than to the Third Temple. The final and permanent temple may not be the Third Temple but another fake one that will ultimately be destroyed, like the two before it.

The final temple, or the Third Temple, will be massive. The Second Temple was only 500 by 500 cubits. The Third Temple, however, will measure 3,000 by 3,000 cubits—approximately 512 acres, roughly the size of Old Jerusalem, a city built as a perfect square.

Revelation 21:1-2 states:

> *And I saw a new heaven and a new earth: for the first heaven and the first earth were passed away; and there was no more sea. (2) And I saw the holy city, the New Jerusalem, coming down out of heaven from God, having been prepared as a bride adorned for her husband.*

Similarly, in Daniel 7:13, we read: *"I saw in the night visions, and, behold, one like the Son of man came with the clouds of heaven, and came to the Ancient of Days, and they brought him near before him."*

Jewish eschatology interprets this as a reference to the Messiah bringing the New Jerusalem or the Third Temple down to earth.

The Ark of the Covenant is said to be in heaven but could also exist on earth in a *tzim tzum*. I do not believe that the Ark has been destroyed or lost forever. It will reappear—whether in heaven, on earth, or both simultaneously. The Ark's physical form may pass away when this natural world does, but the Spirit behind the Ark will endure forever. That Spirit dwells within us and is present wherever the Spirit of God resides.

Although I believe in the Trinity, I cannot fully explain it; yet, I hold it as truth. The same applies to *tzim tzum*. We do not call the Trinity a contradiction but a paradox. Webster's Dictionary defines a paradox as:

"A logically self-contradictory statement or one that runs contrary to expectation. It is a statement that, despite valid reasoning from true premises, leads to a seemingly self-contradictory conclusion."

To say the Trinity is three Gods in one God is a contradiction. But to say the Trinity is three persons in one God is a paradox.

Similarly, saying the Transfiguration took place simultaneously in heaven and on earth could be seen as a contradiction. However, if Moses and Elijah—who were in heaven—existed within a Divine bubble created by Jesus to connect the physical and spiritual realms, it becomes a paradox.

Why was it necessary for Peter, James, and John to witness Jesus conversing with Moses and Elijah? According to the *Likkutei Sichot* (Volume XI, pages 8-13), there is an "inner connection between Moses and the Messiah: The Messiah will be brought by the powers transmitted through Moses." While Moses initiated the Giving of the Torah to purify Israel and the world, the Messiah's task is to complete this process and introduce the subsequent service when the world's purity is complete.

In *Tanya* (Part IV, Chapter 4), it is taught: *"Just as the Torah (through Moses) gives the world the power to bring the Messiah, so it gives every individual the power to refine their own life and environment, hastening the Messianic Age."*

Genesis 49:10 says: *"The scepter shall not depart from Judah, nor a lawgiver from between his feet, until Shiloh come; and unto him shall the gathering of the people be."*

Tanya (Part I, Chapter 43) explains:

> *'Shiloh come' is taken to refer to the Messiah, as the words yavo Shiloh (Shiloh come) and Mashiach (Messiah) are numerically equivalent. This equivalence also applies to the words Shiloh and Moses, showing the coming of the Messiah is related to Moses. Additionally, yavo (come) shares the same numerical value as echad (one). Thus, Messiah = Moses + One.*

I have found that throughout Jewish teachings and literature, "the coming of the Messiah is related to Moses." It is also taught that Elijah will herald the coming of the Messiah. We believe this refers to John the Baptist, which I agree is a picture of the Messiah. However, the Jews believe Elijah will come not only to announce the Messiah but also to denounce false Messiahs.

In Revelation 11:3, we learn about two witnesses: *"And I will give power unto my two witnesses, and they shall prophesy a thousand two hundred and threescore days, clothed in sackcloth."*

These witnesses are not identified, but some say they are Enoch and Elijah, while others believe they are simply two witnesses of that time period. I would suggest that these two witnesses are Moses and Elijah, who come to earth. My personal theory is that they dwell in a *tzim tzum*—a heavenly, non-corrupt body like the one that appeared with Jesus on the Mount of Transfiguration. However, when they come to earth, they take on a body like the one Jesus had after His resurrection. As long as they remain in that *tzim tzum,* no one can harm them. But then God permits them to leave the *tzim tzum,* and their bodies die.

The idea is that a heavenly body cannot exist in our earthly realm without leaving the heavenly realm, and an earthly, corruptible, sinful body cannot exist in a heavenly realm. Jesus is the only one who could exist both in the physical realm in a corruptible body—a body made up of blood cells, skin, and organs that can decay and die—and also exist in a heavenly realm. Jesus was able to move in and out of the *tzim tzum* without His physical body dying.

The next chapter will explore what happens when a physical body is not inhabited by a Divine Spirit, as it was with Jesus. In theology, we talk about the paradox of the incarnation of Jesus—how it is possible for Him to be both God and man at the same time. This is not a contradiction but a paradox, one of the great mysteries of Christianity.

In Hebrews 2:7, we learn that Jesus was made *"a little lower than the angels."* Philippians 2:7-11 further teaches that Jesus *"emptied Himself."* This concept can be used to explain or picture *tzim tzum.* The idea of *tzim tzum,* though not found in the Bible, is a term from extra-biblical literature in Classical Hebrew. In these texts, *'or ein sof* (the Infinite Light) had to be reduced or constricted for God to create the universe. Essentially, God had to establish a *tzim tzum* to create the physical universe, which is like a dark bubble in the center of the *'or ein sof.*

Light, in this context, may serve as a metaphor rather than a literal reference to illumination. We do not fully understand light itself, but we know it is energy that produces wave patterns. When Jesus said, "I am the Light of the world," He may not have been referring to a glowing object but to the essence of all existence and life. He is the gateway and doorway between the physical realm and the supernatural realms.

God says in Deuteronomy 30:15, *"See, I have set before you this day life and good and death and evil."*

89

Jewish teachers often reference this verse to illustrate *tzim tzum.* God had to step aside to create the physical world. Yet, if God were not present in it, the world would be entirely evil and out of harmony with Him.

This may explain the flood narrative. Genesis 6:8 tells us, *"Noah found grace in the eyes of the Lord."* Before the flood, it appears God withdrew His *tzim tzum,* leaving humanity to search for Him. The problem was that without the presence of God's *tzim tzum,* all that remained was evil. Humanity, without divine restraint, chose evil over good. God extended a special grace to Noah, enabling him to seek and find God. After the flood, this special grace became part of human nature, passed down through generations, much like the sin nature.

Without this special grace, humankind was left without restraint, unable to choose what is right. Today, even with the ability to choose right, humanity confuses evil for good and good for evil. For example, some Middle Eastern terrorists believe that killing innocent people is righteous and pleasing to God. This mirrors the time of Noah, when humanity chose evil despite having the ability to choose good. Matthew 24:37 states, *"But as the days of Noah were, so shall also the coming of the Son of man be."*

How does this relate to the *Divine Kiss?* In the *Divine Kiss,* we will be caught up in a *tzim tzum,* similar to Peter, James, and John on the Mount of Transfiguration. In this bubble of *tzim tzum,* we will face no evil whatsoever and experience only the Divine Love—the *racham* of God. In this state, we will be protected by the *tzim tzum,* and our spirit will no longer want to remain in our physical body. It will pass without pain or fear. As 1 John 4:18 says, *"Perfect love casts out all fear."*

This perfect love, experienced within the *tzim tzum,* will bring us into a state of complete harmony with God, free from the fears and limitations of the physical realm.

14. CONQUERING THE FEAR OF DEATH

"For the indignation of the LORD is upon all nations, and his fury upon all their armies: he hath utterly destroyed them, he hath delivered them to the slaughter." (Isaiah 34:2)

Jonathan Edwards lived from 1703 to 1758. He was a theologian, intellectual, and evangelist. After graduating from Yale University and Divinity School, he traveled widely as an evangelist. He is credited with ushering in the Great Awakening in 1733. He pastored churches, preached, and lectured throughout the American colonies. A truly anointed man of God, Edwards brought many into the Kingdom of God. He remains a hero of the faith for many in the Evangelical community.

Edwards eventually became the third president of Princeton University in 1758, succeeding his son-in-law Aaron Burr, the grandson of the Aaron Burr who became vice president of the United States. Edwards was a strong proponent of the smallpox vaccine and encouraged others to take it by leading by example. In 1758, he took the vaccine himself and, according to medical records, died of smallpox shortly thereafter.

This shows that even our heroes are not infallible. To many people, it seemed like madness to take a vaccine with a live virus to prevent the disease, as the early smallpox vaccine required. Today, we use dead viruses to achieve the same immunity. Edwards was so revered as a man of God that the intellectual community convinced him his actions would save thousands, perhaps even hundreds of thousands. Unfortunately, we see how that played out. While I greatly admire Jonathan Edwards and his achievements, he, like all of us, had feet of clay. Not everything he did was perfect, and his choices are open to question.

One of Edwards' most famous sermons, delivered on July 8, 1741, at age 38, is titled *"Sinners in the Hands of an Angry God."* This sermon has become emblematic of fire-and-brimstone preaching, though Edwards' original delivery was soft-spoken, gentle, and compassionate. Unlike modern animated preachers, his words carried their own weight without resorting to horror or alarm. The word *angry* in Edwards' time did not necessarily carry the same emotional intensity it does today. Three hundred years ago, it often conveyed strong annoyance or displeasure rather than hostility.

While fire-and-brimstone sermons have scared many into salvation, I find it hard to believe in a God so irrationally angry that He would destroy someone for breaking a rule in a moment of wrath. I once heard a preacher say, "You have nothing to fear from God's love—but you had better be afraid of God." While anger may inspire fear, this fear seems at odds with 1 John 4:18, *"There is no fear in love; but perfect love casteth out fear: because fear hath torment. He that feareth is not made perfect in love."*

The Greek word for *fear* here is *phobos,* which is where we get the English word *phobia.* It conveys the idea of withdrawing out of fear of consequences. In Aramaic, the word *dachalatha'* (from the root *dachal*) carries a similar meaning. Interestingly, *dachal* is also the root for the word used for scarecrows—non-living objects that frighten birds into avoiding cultivated areas. Thus, both *phobos* and *dachal* suggest a protective fear, one meant to warn and preserve.

Why should we fear death? After all, the promise of a heavenly home—with streets of gold, pearly gates, and eternal peace—sounds far more appealing than the struggles of this earthly life. No more pain, anxiety, or political strife—just harmony and rest. What stops us from hastening our departure to this better existence?

God placed a natural *dachal*—a fear of death—within us. While it may seem unreasonable in light of eternity, this fear serves a purpose. Without it, we might abandon our earthly lives at the first sign of trouble, failing to fulfill the purpose for which God placed us here.

This fear also enhances our experiences. For example, skydivers often describe a mix of terror and exhilaration. A former student who was an Airborne Ranger once told me about his first jump. His jumpmaster assured him the parachute would open 99.9% of the time. Yet, standing at the door of a plane two miles above the ground, he couldn't help but think, "What if I'm that 0.1%?" The rush of adrenaline upon jumping, however, created an unbelievable high. Overcoming fear can bring a profound sense of accomplishment and joy.

1 John 4:18 teaches that perfect love casts out all fear. The Greek word for *cast out* is *exo* (outside) and *ballei* (to throw), painting a picture of tossing fear far away from oneself. In Aramaic, the word *shua* means to expel, eject, or excommunicate. In this verse, the verb is in the intensive *Pael* form, emphasizing the complete and total elimination of fear.

The context of this verse speaks to death. The perfect love of God expels all fear of death. Most of us have not yet fully experienced this perfect love—this *chav,* or human love, perfected into *racham,* the divine love of God. However, as we draw closer to God, this fear begins to fade. By the time God calls us home, *chav* has transformed into perfect *racham,* allowing us to experience the joy and euphoria of release.

This moment of transition is what Jewish tradition calls the *Divine Kiss.* It is the culmination of God's perfect love, freeing us from all fear as we enter His eternal presence.

15. WHAT DID STEPHEN SEE?

*But he, being full of the Holy Ghost, looked up steadfastly into heav-
en, and saw the glory of God, and Jesus standing on the right hand
of God, And said, Behold, I see the heavens opened, and the Son of
man standing on the right hand of God.* (Acts 7:55-56)

Stephen was preaching a truly anointed sermon to members of the Sanhedrin, and the Holy Spirit was strongly convicting them. I recall conducting an online class when a group of people hacked in. They began
mocking us, using every vulgar and racist word they could to disrupt
the discussion. Such hatred was being expressed toward a discussion
about the love of God. Why would speaking of love elicit such hatred?
Of course, this could have been demonically generated, but it could also
have been the convicting power of the Holy Spirit.

Many have followed the trials of a former television star who faced hatred
and anger for simply reading a portion of his children's book about love,
acceptance, and family in a public library. Protesters not only demanded
the book be banned but also opposed the banning of sexually explicit
books targeted at children. They argued that forbidding a child from
being exposed to adult sexual situations was an expression of hate. Was
this demonically generated? Perhaps—or perhaps it was the convicting
power of the Holy Spirit.

As a pastor, I once shared the message of Jesus with a young woman who desperately wanted to accept Him as her Savior. She admitted her desire but said she simply could not do it. She was under such conviction by the Holy Spirit that she was literally shaking, breaking out in a cold sweat. Using an ancient idiom, we might say she was "gnashing her teeth." She confessed she was living with her boyfriend, unmarried, and feared that accepting the Lord would require her to stop living with him—and likely to break up with him, as he was not a Christian.

It turned out her boyfriend was also under conviction by the Holy Spirit. After this woman accepted the Lord, her boyfriend called me and asked for a visit. He wanted to invite Jesus into his heart, as did his young son. A couple of months later, I performed their wedding. The convicting power of the Holy Spirit can evoke a wide range of emotional responses, from pure hatred to fear and even to gnashing of teeth.

Why were the distinguished priests and high priests of the temple so upset with Stephen, a young upstart they labeled a heretic? After all, dealing with heretics was part of their job. The priests acted as the Executive Branch of their religious system, and the Sanhedrin served as the Judicial Branch. Their role was to decide whether religious laws were violated. If someone was declared guilty of breaking religious law and refused to repent, the response was often described as "gnashing of teeth."

The Aramaic word for gnashing is *charam*, not to be confused with the Hebrew word spelled the same way, which means total or utter destruction. In Aramaic, *charam* conveys total or utter rejection. It has the idea of cutting with one's teeth, symbolizing being cut off from fellowship. It is a term for excommunication. When used as a verb with the nominative "teeth," it becomes an idiomatic expression of grinding one's teeth in frustration, complaining loudly and angrily. This idiom conveys the sense of being so angry at someone that one wants to lash out but restrains oneself. Instead, the person is shunned or excommunicated.

In the case of Stephen, the priests and Sanhedrin members were gnashing their teeth in frustration and anger. Whether they literally gnashed their teeth or the Scripture uses this phrase idiomatically to indicate their rejection of Stephen, the meaning is clear: at this point, Stephen was being excommunicated.

By the first century, the Jewish people had endured centuries of captivity and foreign rule, which left them weary of executions. Though the Torah prescribed capital punishment for six offenses, the Sanhedrin had established numerous checks, balances, appeals, and rules that made such sentences exceedingly rare.

For instance, consider the story of the woman caught in adultery, brought before Jesus. According to Torah law, if a woman was caught in adultery, she was to be put to death. However, the oral law, which Jesus often critiqued, introduced due process. The Pharisees brought this woman to Jesus not because He had the authority to execute her, but to trap Him. They hoped He would either disregard Torah law or validate their oral traditions, which they believed added fairness and compassion.

Instead, Jesus turned their argument on its head. When He stooped to write on the ground, many speculate He wrote either a *yod* or *Yod Hei Yod*—an abbreviation for God's name in feminine form, appealing to God's mercy. Then He declared, "Let him who is without sin cast the first stone." In essence, He challenged them: if anyone here is so righteous that they do not need God's mercy, let them pass judgment.

Jesus highlighted their hypocrisy, emphasizing that true justice must include God's mercy and forgiveness. After the accusers left, Jesus told the woman, *"Go and sin no more."* Her repentance meant she was forgiven by God, and if God forgives, so must we. Importantly, true repentance requires turning away from sin.

Stephen's message to the Pharisees and priests should not have resulted in such a violent reaction, let alone a demand for the death penalty. It deeply upset them, but they were religious men and tried to restrain themselves, gnashing their teeth in frustration and excommunicating Stephen from the temple. Excommunication meant total rejection—being cut off from fellowship, banned from the temple, and shunned from all synagogues. Stephen would not have been allowed to teach, and anyone listening to or embracing his teaching would also face excommunication.

Why were these typically peaceful members of the priesthood so enraged that they sought Stephen's death? Was it demonic influence or the convicting power of the Holy Spirit? Accepting Stephen's message would have jeopardized their positions in the temple and demanded a personal

cost. Just as the woman who feared accepting Jesus because of the sacrifices involved, these temple leaders would have had to pay a price for
accepting Stephen's words. Yet, his message was so convicting that they
could not bear to listen—they felt it pierce the very core of their hearts.

The murderous intent only arose when Stephen described a vision he
experienced. At that point, they dragged him outside the city to stone
him. Even then, the stoning was only carried out under the authority of
a key Sanhedrin member, Saul (later Paul), who had judicial power to
authorize executions. This suggests a level of premeditated collaboration
between the Sanhedrin and the High Priest, much like the collaboration
that led to Jesus' arrest.

What did Stephen see that enraged the priests so greatly? He described
seeing two things: the glory of God and Jesus standing at God's right
hand. For the priests, this was blasphemy, as it suggested two Gods—a
violation of Judaism's foundational creed that there is only one God. But
Stephen's vision was not a challenge to monotheism; he saw the glory of
God, and within that glory, he experienced Jesus—Yahshua, meaning
"Salvation"—standing at the right hand of God.

The word "glory" in Aramaic in this passage is *tashakuchatha*, derived
from the root *shakach*. This feminine form emphasizes God's mercy, compassion, love, and care—an expression of *racham*, God's perfect, heavenly
love. This is the same glory Moses sought in Exodus 33:18 when he asked
God, *"Now show me your glory."* God responded in verse 19, describing
His glory not with the word *kebode* (glory), but through His goodness
(*tov*), grace (*chanan*), and mercy (*racham*).

God's *tov* refers to the harmonious vibrations of His perfect nature,
which sustain all creation. Moses' sinful, corrupted flesh could not with-
stand such harmony. God's *chanan* is His divine favor, extended through
a blood covenant—a relationship akin to the "blood brothers" ritual seen
in old Western stories. Finally, *racham* represents God's perfect, heavenly
love, which transcends human understanding.

God explained to Moses that seeing His face (*pani*—often a reference
to His presence) would cause Moses' spirit to leave his body and join
God. Essentially, God was telling Moses, "What you are asking for is my

Divine Kiss. Although we both long for it, it cannot happen until your earthly mission is complete."

Stephen's vision of God's glory—His *shakach*—was an overwhelming experience of seeing, feeling, hearing, smelling, and tasting all at once. This type of perception defies physical understanding, as it transcends the limitations of our five senses. The Aramaic word *chaza'*, used for "see," implies perceiving or experiencing rather than mere physical sight.

When Stephen said he saw Jesus standing at the right hand of God, he was describing an encounter with the omnipotence of God. The "right hand" is a metaphor for divine power, honor, and priority. In that moment, Stephen experienced the fullness of God's presence (*pani*), His favor (*chanan*), His heavenly love (*racham*), and His perfect harmony (*tov*), all wrapped in the glory of God.

Did Stephen see Jesus physically, or was it a manifestation? It is unclear, as experiencing the spirit world with unified senses is beyond our comprehension. Stephen likely recognized Jesus by divine revelation, even though he may not have met Him during His earthly ministry.

The Pharisees and priests, however, could not discern the spiritual nature of Stephen's vision. They only understood his words as heretical, implying two Gods. This was enough for them to condemn him to death.

Remarkably, God allowed Stephen to see His glory before his physical death. The process of dying began before the first stone was thrown. In this way, God granted Stephen the experience that Moses had longed for: to witness His glory while still in a physical body. By the time the stoning began, Stephen was already resting safely in the arms of God, having received the *Divine Kiss*. Even as his body functioned enough to utter the words "Father, forgive them," Stephen's spirit was united with God, untouched by pain or fear.

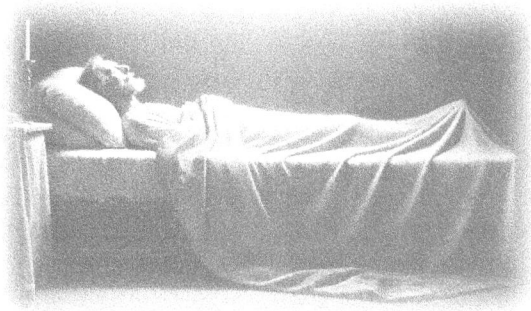

16. PRAYING FOR THE DIVINE KISS

I had fainted, unless I had believed to see the goodness of the LORD in the land of the living. (14) Wait on the LORD: be of good courage, and he shall strengthen thine heart: wait, I say, on the LORD. (Psalm 27:13-14)

"The land of the living." What a curious phrase for the Psalmist to use. Why does he specifically want to see the goodness of God in the land of the living? And why does he follow this with an admonition to wait on the Lord, to be of good courage, and to strengthen one's heart? He repeats: wait on the Lord. The tone of the Psalm suggests the writer is facing urgent danger and needs help immediately. Yet, he speaks of waiting. Is it really deliverance from trouble that the Psalmist is waiting for, or is he expressing a deeper longing?

A careful reading of the Psalm reveals the Psalmist's desire to dwell in the house of the Lord, seek Him in His temple, and hide in His shelter. These statements hint at a dual meaning—finding rest in the presence of God during one's earthly life and ultimately resting in His eternal embrace. The imagery speaks to both the natural and the supernatural realms.

The word "wait" in this passage is *qavah*, which originates from the Akkadian language, meaning twisting or turning, creating tension. It conveys the idea of enduring. The Psalmist does not imply passively waiting for

God's intervention; instead, he describes an active endurance, holding on tightly to God until help arrives.

Tracing *qavah* further into its Semitic roots, the term relates to rope-making. Ancient ropes were created by binding hundreds of individual strands tightly together, forming a strong, unbreakable cord. This process demonstrates the strength that comes from unity. In the same way, *qavah* implies binding oneself so tightly to God that no force can sever the connection. Like a window washer trusting his life to a securely woven rope, the believer is bound to God with an unshakable bond of trust and dependence.

Why does the Psalmist emphasize "the land of the living"? At first glance, it seems to refer to the natural world. However, the Hebrew word for "living" here is *chaim*, which is plural. If the Psalmist were speaking solely of earthly life, he would have used the singular form, *chai*. The plural form suggests something beyond the physical—a duality of existence encompassing both earthly life and spiritual life.

Jewish midrash teaches that the plural form of "life" signifies two realms of existence: our life here on earth and our life in the spiritual realm with God. Thus, the Psalmist is making a plea not only for earthly deliverance but also for the continuation of his bond with God in eternity.

The Psalmist's desire to be so *qavah*—so tightly bound to God—implies that as he transitions from earthly life, his bond with God remains unbroken. His anxieties, sufferings, and earthly attachments may fall away, but his connection to God will persist unchanged. For the Psalmist, nothing else matters as much as this eternal bond.

The Psalmist's attitude mirrors the sentiments expressed in Rusty Goodman's song *I've Got Leavin' On My Mind*:

> *I guess I should be looking for a better place to live.*
> *But I can't seem to get excited about this world and what it can give.*
> *I couldn't care less if I could buy it all with a solitary dime.*
> *What good would a world down here do me, with leaving on my mind?*

Similarly, the Apostle Paul wrote in Romans 8:38-39:

> *For I am persuaded, that neither death, nor life, nor angels, nor principalities, nor powers, nor things present, nor things to come, Nor height, nor depth, nor any other creature, shall be able to separate us from the love of God, which is in Christ Jesus our Lord.*

Paul, once a powerful and wealthy member of the Sanhedrin, lost everything—his position, wealth, influence, and likely even his marriage—after his encounter with Christ. Despite losing it all, he found fulfillment in his bond with God, declaring that nothing could separate him from the love of God in Christ. The Psalmist expresses a similar sentiment in Psalm 27, seeking to be so closely bound to God that even the loss of life itself is inconsequential compared to the enduring love of God.

The Psalmist's longing points to the *Divine Kiss*—the moment of ultimate union with God upon leaving this earthly life. Importantly, this is a longing that can and should be expressed in prayer even now. Moses, too, prayed for the *Divine Kiss* when he asked to see God's glory. While God denied Moses' request at that time, Moses eventually received the *Divine Kiss* when his earthly mission was complete.

Can we pray for the *Divine Kiss* for ourselves or others? Absolutely. In fact, we are encouraged to comfort those nearing the end of life by reminding them of the promise of the *Divine Kiss*. Jesus' model prayer, the Lord's Prayer, emphasizes communal prayer:

> *"Our Father" (not "my Father"),*
> *"Give us our daily bread" (not "give me"),*
> *"Lead us not into temptation" (not "lead me").*

This communal focus extends to praying for our brothers and sisters in Christ, especially those facing death. We can pray that they receive the *Divine Kiss* and find peace in God's presence, reminding them of the love and eternal bond they have with Him.

Many years ago, I was an assistant pastor in a church that had four different types of Christians. First, there were the fundamentalists who were very evangelistic. They believed we should be out there winning souls and, above all, fighting against the rising tide of a new movement called the charismatic movement. These charismatic Christians made up one-fourth of the church membership. These were members who grew up in the church but got caught up in this new movement of Pentecostalism, which, thanks to the Jesus movement, was infiltrating all the mainline churches. These people believed in miracles, faith healing, and—good grief—speaking in tongues.

The fundamentalists were determined to force all these charismatic people (or "crazy people," as we called them behind their backs) out of the church. Another quarter of the church was made up of rank liberals—denominational worshippers who accepted everything their liberal denomination taught, including guest speakers and programs provided by the denomination. These were the ones who prayed every day facing Dallas, Texas (home of the denominational headquarters).

Finally, there was the fourth group, making up the last quarter of the church, who were my biggest supporters. These were the good, faithful, tithing people who believed in God but were essentially Sunday-only Christians. They attended church on Sunday and lived the rest of the week like everyone else. They didn't care about theology, evangelism, or tongues and couldn't even tell you the name of their denomination. To them, the church was the poor man's country club.

So, here I was, fresh out of seminary, ready to be your pious parish pastor, conducting funerals, weddings, visiting people in the hospital, and giving invocations at community events. Yet, I found myself acting as a referee between the four factions that were constantly at each other's throats.

One day, I received a phone call from one of the "crazy" people, who told me her elderly neighbor was in hospice care and had been brought home to die. It appeared her time had come, and her husband asked for a preacher to be present.

"Wow, was I excited! Finally, I could start doing some real preacher stuff—the things I was trained to do in seminary. No more mediating disputes over tongues, healing, virgin births, inspiration of the Bible, or trying to maintain peace and prevent the church from splitting into four. I grabbed my book of prayers, my Bible with all the key verses on death and dying underlined, dressed in my best preacher suit, and headed over to do my best Bing Crosby Father Flanagan imitation.

I arrived to find an elderly woman, mentally disconnected from the world but physically restless in her hospital bed—tossing, turning, ranting, and raving, all while upsetting her grieving husband. When I entered, her husband ran to me and begged, "Oh, preacher, thank God you're here. You have to pray, preacher; you have to pray. Look at her—my poor wife is suffering so. Oh, please, preacher, pray!"

Unfortunately, he didn't specify how I should pray. I walked up to the hospital bed, leaned toward the woman who had called me to come over, and whispered, "I don't know what to pray. She's in her 90s; she's going to die. Should I pray she be healed, or what?" The charismatic woman quietly said, "I think I know how to pray." I told her to please go ahead.

She placed her hand on the woman's forehead and began to pray in a language I didn't recognize. When she finished, I asked, "Do you know what you prayed?" She replied, "No, but whatever it was, it was right." And indeed, whatever that "gobbledy-gook" was, it got results.

Suddenly, the woman—who had been moments earlier ranting and raving in delirium—became quiet and peaceful. A glowing smile came over her face. My first thought was, "Oh no, we killed her." But she was still breathing—quietly and regularly now. Her husband slapped me on the back, shook my hand, and said, "Boy, you preachers sure know how to pray, all right! Look at her—so peaceful and relaxed, even smiling." I said, "No, it wasn't me; it was—uh..."

I later learned this dying woman was truly a born-again Christian who often spoke of her love for God throughout her life. Later that day, I received word that she had passed peacefully from this life—with that glowing smile still on her face.

Well, who wouldn't smile after being kissed by God? Sometimes, we're called to the bedside of a loved one simply to remind them that, as they approach their final breath, it will be to return that breath of life to the God who gave it to them in the first place. And He will receive that final breath with a kiss—the *Divine Kiss*.

17. PREPARING FOR THE DIVINE KISS

Who shall separate us from the love of Christ? Shall tribulation, or distress, or persecution, or famine, or nakedness, or peril, or sword? As it is written, For thy sake we are killed all the day long; we are accounted as sheep for the slaughter. Nay, in all these things we are more than conquerors through him that loved us. For I am persuaded that neither death, nor life, nor angels, nor principalities, nor powers, nor things present, nor things to come, Nor height, nor depth, nor any other creature, shall be able to separate us from the love of God, which is in Christ Jesus our Lord. Romans 8:35-39)

I am not only old enough to remember the Berlin Wall coming down, I remember when it was first erected. After World War II defeated Germany in 1945, the nation was divided into Soviet, American, British, and French zones of occupation. The city of Berlin, though technically part of the Soviet zone, was also split, with the Soviets taking the eastern blockade. Things were so bad in the Soviet sector that over the next 12 years, between 2.5 million and 3 million citizens of East Germany headed to democratic West Germany. The drain included many professional and skilled workers, such that on August 13, 1961, the Soviets erected a wall to keep its citizens from leaving. The communists began a purge of all dissenters, including Christians.

I recall, even as an eleven-year-old child, hearing an interview of a young woman who escaped from East Germany to the West. She described the horrors of living under the communistic regime. She told how a group of soldiers entered a café and confronted her and her Christian friends who were reading the Bible. One soldier grabbed her, threw her against a wall, and began to mercilessly beat her, demanding she renounce her faith in God and submit to the communist rule. She refused to deny her Jesus as he continued to beat her until she fell bloody and unconscious.

The reporter asked her why she endured such a beating and would not just say a few words denouncing her faith, which would have saved her from the beating. Even at the age of eleven years old, her reply has haunted me after all these years. She simply said with a heavy German accent: "Because I love Jesus." Those words of this beautiful young woman who was beaten into unconsciousness simply because she wanted to love her Jesus were imprinted in my very soul such that even today, after over half a century of walking with my Savior, I can still hear those heavily accented words: "Because I love Jesus."

I have long stopped wondering if my love for Jesus would extend that far if I should ever find myself in a similar situation. I realize that all the trials and temptations I have been through over my life have been used by God as kindling to light that fiery passion of His love, which will one day culminate in a *Divine Hug* followed by a *Divine Kiss* when I pass from this world into the arms of the God I love. After walking this earth for 73 years, I've learned that maybe at this moment I don't think I would take such a stand for my faith. Yet, I am confident that should such a moment come, God will give me what I need to take that stand.

I am convinced and persuaded that should a time like that ever come, what I will need is an overwhelming sense of God's presence and love—a love that transcends anything this physical world can offer, such that even facing the end of our own physical existence in this world would be of little consequence compared to basking in that racham love for eternity. Even now, He is preparing me for what my grandpa used to call "that great gettin' up mornin'."

The Apostle Paul had everything this life could offer. He had power, wealth, influence, respect, honor—all the things one spends their life pursuing—and not only that, but Paul had this as a young man. He was a Roman citizen by birth, which means he was a man of wealth. He was a distinguished member of the Sanhedrin, a sort of Jewish Supreme Religious Court.

Then one day, he met that love—that powerful racham love of Jesus—and experienced His fond embrace. This is something that the Jews call devekut, a *Divine Hug*, which will be explained in a later study. This love was so powerful, so overwhelming, that Paul left his idyllic life behind to become an itinerant preacher who was chased out of towns, stoned, beaten, shipwrecked, imprisoned, and eventually executed by the Romans for his newfound faith in Jesus. Apparently, in spite of all this trouble and loss, he never looked back. We know this from his declaration in Romans 8:35-39.

He starts off this declaration in Romans 8:35 with: *"Who can separate us from the love of Christ?"* In the Aramaic, the pronoun *who* is *ma'n,* which means *who* or *what.* The context would suggest both *who* and *what,* as this would apparently include non-persons, that is, circumstances as well as individuals. *Who or what shall separate us?*

The word *separate* in the Aramaic is *parash,* which means to separate in the sense of causing one to avoid or keep away from something—causing someone to avoid contact with someone or something. This is in a Pael active form, so it is not Paul saying that something or someone could cause him to avoid or come in contact with God's love, but that nothing can keep God from loving or coming in contact with him.

It is interesting that this word *love* is *chav* and not *racham. Chav* is a love that exists in the natural realm, and that is the most God can give us while we are in this natural, corrupt body. Once we leave this body, we will enter into the fullness of the love called *racham.* Yet, the word *chav* in Aramaic is *chavah,* which is in an emphatic form. This is the ultimate expression of love that we in this physical realm and body can experience. It is a love experience from God that we cannot experience through anything else this world has to offer.

Paul then lists the many things that one might believe could cause God to separate His love from us but, in reality, will not. Tribulation is listed. This is something Paul knew quite well during his ministry. Tribulation is the word *'alatz* in Aramaic, which is also emphatic and means intense hardship, calamity, oppression, affliction, distress, and suffering. In the midst of all this, God's love can be found.

To be robbed by bandits in the middle of a desert was almost a death sentence. One can only imagine the horror of being robbed, stripped naked, and left in the middle of a desert with little to no hope of obtaining any other garments. Yet, even in this, one can still find the love of God in Christ Jesus. Paul knew and could testify to that fact.

Paul faced many perils and the sword. The word peril is *qanadinvus*, which is a very dangerous situation, and the word sword is *siph*, which means the threat of death or death by sword, or what we would say today as the threat of death by a dangerous weapon.

It was no vacation to go on a missionary journey in those days. I recall attending a large church where the senior pastor was invited to take a missionary journey to a foreign land. Special offerings were taken to pay his plane fare and cover the cost of sleeping in a five-star hotel while he was wined and dined by the brethren who practically held him up as some hero. He slept in a comfortable bed protected by hotel security and was watched over by a police force as he toured the sights of the land to send back reports of his sacrificial efforts to reach the people of this lost land. He then had adoring crowds gather to hear this American preach. Oh, how we honored this man of God for his sacrifice. What a servant of God he was to leave his comfortable home to travel to distant lands, which he proudly displayed on his Facebook page and discussed in his latest book. That experience was worlds apart from Paul's missionary experience.

Paul could truly sing that old hymn to be written over 1600 years later:

"Through many dangers, toils, and snares, I have already come;
'Tis grace hath brought me safe thus far,
And grace will lead me home." —John Newton (Public Domain)

Yet, through all his trials, the love of God followed him, and he never looked back. He was able to testify that "In all these things, we are more than conquerors through him that loved us." The words "In all these things" are one Aramaic word, *bahalin*, which translates to "in all of this." In other words, despite all these things that took place, Paul was able to testify that he was more than a conqueror. The word for conqueror is *zakar*, which literally means a righteous victor. We come through all these trials victorious without lowering ourselves to anything unrighteous. It is through Him who loved us. But note that the word love is *dahachavan*, which literally means "through all this, He has kindled His love." It is not only His love that brings us through all these things, but these things are what help kindle—that is, light or start—that fire of His love. The more we endure for the sake of the Kingdom of God, the greater the love of God increases in us to bring us through it all.

After years of going through the fires of trials and difficulties, God is lighting a fire of His passionate love in us such that by the time He is ready to bring us home, we will be so overwhelmed in His love that at the moment, or even before that moment, we will receive that *Divine Kiss*.

Thus, nothing in death nor life, nor angels, will separate us from the love of God. The word angels in Aramaic is *maleka*, which refers to good angels who are messengers. Sometimes the message of angels is not all that exciting, as Paul found out in Acts 27:23-24: *"For there stood by me this night the angel of God, whose I am, and whom I serve, Saying, Fear not, Paul; thou must be brought before Caesar: and, lo, God hath given thee all them that sail with thee."*

He was basically telling Paul that things may have been bad before, but now they will get worse—he will have to appear before Caesar and, on the way, will be shipwrecked. But at least the angel assured him of God's protective love. Still, you know, sometimes you wonder if it is better not to know the future. But not even the message of angels or principalities—which Bible scholars agree mean demonic messengers—and powers, which are a reference to human governments seeking to force you to denounce your faith, can cause the love of God to be hindered. Neither can things present—any message you receive in the present, like a bad medical report from the doctor—or the future, like the treatment you need to take as a result of that bad report, separate you from the love of God.

Paul declared he was persuaded. That word in Aramaic for persuaded is *maphas*, which is the breaking of one's will. Through all that Paul went through, suffered through, and experienced, God broke his will to the point where he was ready to submit to whatever was dished out to him. He had the confidence that no matter what it was, even facing the sword that lopped his head off, it never separated him from the love of God.

Neither height nor depth. This is a first-century idiom for the totality of something. Neither height nor depth nor any creature. The word creature is *bara'*, which refers to anything created. Thus, Paul is saying that nothing in this physical universe that was created by God can separate him from the love of God, which is in Christ Jesus.

Paul's experience with the *Divine Kiss* started long before he faced the executioner's sword. God was *dahachavan* with Paul—that is, kindling the love of God, fanning the flames of His *chav* love, preparing him for that final moment when the executioner dropped his sword. By that time, Paul was already in a state of *devekut*, in the arms of God, receiving a *Divine Kiss*, feeling no fear, just great anticipation of entering the fullness of God's *racham* love.

This morning, I was at my favorite place in the park meditating on Romans 8:35-39 as I was waiting for the sun to rise. I suddenly felt God speak to me, saying: "You fully expected My sun to rise, yet My love is more certain than that." Even now, with every trial, every heartbreak, every struggle, God is kindling that *ahav* love in you, preparing you for the *devekut*, Divine Hug, to give you the *Divine Kiss*.

18. THE DIVINE HUG II

"I will both lie down in peace, and sleep; For You alone, O LORD, make me dwell in safety." (Psalm 4:8)

"I will both lie down in peace?" That sounds a bit odd. What is this "both?" Many commentators say the word "both" really means "at the same time." The Psalmist is resting and at peace simultaneously. I can accept that, but I think it means more than that. The word for "both" is *yichud,* which means "together" and "united." God and the Psalmist lie together in peace and safety. But among ancient Jews—and even today—*yichud* means much, much more.

If you ever attend a Jewish wedding, you will notice that after the bride and groom pass through the *chuppah,* they enter a *Yichud Room* for a brief time. *Yichud* is also a word used for marital love. The most common word for love in Hebrew is *ahav.* This word is used for the love of parents, siblings, friends, your pet dog Sparky, and Big Macs. Yet, although the word *ahav* appears over two hundred times in the Old Testament, it is rarely used with respect to marital love. It is not used for romantic love. When used in a marital relationship, *ahav* is used for comparison. For instance, Jacob loved Rachel more than Leah.

Ultimately, there is only one word for marital love, and that is *yichud,* because in marriage, two become one. There is no other human relationship that fits that description. If a man had two wives, like Elkanah and his wives, Hannah and Peninah, *ahav* is used for comparison to show preference. Elkanah preferred Hannah over Peninah. But in a true sense, he *yichud* only one woman—Hannah.

Abraham loved both Sarah and Hagar; both gave him sons. It was Sarah's idea that Abraham sleep with her handmaid to produce a child. How could a woman—a wife—suggest such a thing? Because Sarah knew that a man could only *yichud* one woman, and she knew that was her. Even if Abraham slept with Hagar and loved her, Sarah understood she was the one Abraham *yichud*. Similarly, Ahasuerus loved Esther above all women (Esther 2:17). As a king, he had a harem and many women he could sleep with. However, even though he had many women in his harem, there was only one who could enjoy the privilege of receiving *yichud* from the king.

In Shakespeare's play *Julius Caesar*, we find a beautiful picture of *yichud*. In Act 2, Scene 1, Brutus is brooding over the role he must play in the assassination of his friend Julius Caesar. His wife, Portia, notices how disturbed he is:

Portia:

> *Musing and sighing, with your arms across,*
> *And when I asked you what the matter was,*
> *You stared upon me with ungentle looks.*
> *I urged you further; then you scratched your head*
> *And too impatiently stamped with your foot.*
> *Yet I insisted; yet you answered not,*
> *But with an angry wafture of your hand*
> *Gave sign for me to leave you. So I did,*
> *Fearing to strengthen that impatience*
> *Which seemed too much enkindled, and withal*
> *Hoping it was but an effect of humor,*
> *Which sometime hath his hour with every man."*

Here we have Portia, fully aware of the grief her husband Brutus is experiencing, begging him to share what is troubling him. However, Brutus waves her off, and she presses further:

Portia:

> *You have some sick offense within your mind,*
> *Which by the right and virtue of my place*
> *I ought to know of.*

She kneels:

> *And upon my knees I charm you, by my once-commended beauty,*
> *By all your vows of love, and that great vow*
> *Which did incorporate and make us one,*
> *That you unfold to me, your self, your half,*
> *Why you are heavy, and what men tonight*
> *Have had resort to you; for here have been*
> *Some six or seven who did hide their faces*
> *Even from darkness.*

Now, she is on her knees, pleading with Brutus to share what is troubling his heart. Brutus asks her to stand, but still, he refuses to share his burden. At this point, Portia reveals the depth of her torment over her husband's refusal to confide in her:

Portia:

> *I should not need, if you were gentle Brutus.*
> *Within the bond of marriage, tell me, Brutus,*
> *Is it excepted I should know no secrets*
> *That appertain to you? Am I your self*
> *But, as it were, in sort or limitation,*
> *To keep with you at meals, comfort your bed,*
> *And talk to you sometimes? Dwell I but in the suburbs*
> *Of your good pleasure? If it be no more,*

Portia now lays bare her deepest sorrow, declaring:

Portia:

> *Portia is Brutus' harlot, not his wife.*

The emperors of Rome did not have harems because of the danger of mixing bloodlines. This also applied to noblemen, who avoided extramarital affairs, although slaves were often used for sexual services, as any resulting children would not threaten the line of succession. Yet, Portia saw herself as more than a noblewoman married to one of nobility—she saw herself as a partner, one with her husband. Even if he indulged with a slave, none would share what she shared with her husband: *yichud*.

In fact, after this scene in the play, Portia becomes so grief-stricken over her husband's refusal to share his heart with her that she commits suicide. Portia could not bear what she felt was the loss of the *yichud* between herself and Brutus. Even among pagan societies, there was still the idea of one man to one woman. There was a recognition that a husband and wife were more than just sexual partners. The love between a husband and wife was unique—not just *ahav*, but a love so special that it deserved its own word: *yichud*.

Ahav love most often must be commanded, as in "love your neighbor." Neighbors may not always love you in return, and sometimes loving your neighbor requires almost unnatural effort. There is no demand for intimacy in this love. Yet, *yichud* indicates intimacy—a balanced, mutual relationship. It is a simple love, one that is more lasting and natural. This is the love of a spouse.

Unlike *ahav*, *yichud* suggests both complete and sustained love within a sexual relationship, always within the framework of marriage. *Yichud* is not permitted before marriage and certainly not outside of marriage. This is why it is the name given to the conclusion of the marriage ceremony, where the covenant of marriage is established.

Mystically, *ahav* changes to *yichud* after the ceremony under the *chuppah* when the bride and groom retire to a private room for a brief period. This is called the *Yichud Room*. Only the newly married couple has the key to this room. No one else may enter, and there are no interruptions. In this room, the couple joins together alone to contemplate their new life as one flesh. This moment symbolizes their choice of one another to the exclusion of all others.

This small ritual of entering the *Yichud Room* illustrates that *yichud* love is never to be sought outside the marriage chamber. All future expressions of love must be contained within the marriage chamber, and all tender affection must be directed toward one another.

When the couple passes through the *chuppah,* they are declared to be "born again." In John 3, Jesus tells Nicodemus that one must be born again. Nicodemus, confused, asks how one can be born again. *"Is he to enter his mother's womb again?"* Jesus responds, *"You, a teacher and Jewish scholar, do not understand what it means to be born again?"* What happens when a couple gets married? What do you declare when that couple passes through the *chuppah?* They are literally starting a new life, as two individuals joined as one flesh.

"Nicodemus, can't you see the connection between being married to God and a marriage between a man and woman? When you decide to be married to God, you are entering a new life. When you pass under the *chuppah,* you are no longer living for yourself—your own will, desires, and dreams. You have taken on another, with whom you will share your will, desires, and dreams, modifying them to accommodate the new relationship. It is no longer *your* money but *our* money; no longer *your* house but *our* house; no longer *your* dreams but *our* dreams. So it is when you are married to God."

Yichud implies an old Jewish saying: *"Beito zu ishto—a man's home is his wife."* Why do you think it is called *Beith Yaakov*—House of Jacob, or *Beith Yisrael*—House of Israel? The house and home belong to husband and wife, not just the husband or just the wife. The man's home is not his castle; it is his wife and, eventually, his family. Just as God's home is neither this earth nor heaven, His home is us, and wherever we are is where His home is.

For you see, when we accept Jesus as our Savior, we enter into *yichud* love—a love that is mutual, intimate, private, and a mystery. The mystery is that there is something even greater that awaits us. One day, we shall be truly joined as one with God and will know the next level of love, and that is *racham.*

Now take our study verse, Psalm 4:8: *"I will both lie down in peace, and sleep; For You alone, O LORD, make me dwell in safety."* Substitute the word *both* with the word *yichud,* and what do you have? "I will lie down *yichud* (together with God), united as one, in peace and sleep. For You alone, O Lord, make me dwell in safety."

The word for sleep is *yashan,* which is also a word used for "old" and "weary." When we reach that point in our lives when we become old and weary, we dwell with God in safety. The word for safety is *batach,* which is a word used for welding. When we grow old and weary, we will be so welded with God. When two pieces of metal are welded together, they become one piece. Just as in a marriage, when a bride and groom are married, their love becomes *yichud,* which eventually *batach* them together so they become one.

This is the picture of our relationship with God. When we are saved—born again—we are married to God, but we have not yet consummated that marriage. We are betrothed to Him during our time in this physical realm. However, our love for God becomes *yichud* love—a marital love that longs to be consummated, joined with the other to become one. When we pass from this earth, we enter that *yichud room.*

After many funerals, the mourners meet for a meal and reflect on the life of the departed. It is similar to the feast that takes place at a wedding reception—or, more precisely, the feast at the end of the betrothal period. The bride and groom are not present; they are off in the *yichud room,* oblivious to the reception, just as the reception continues when the bride and groom sneak out on their honeymoon. Their only concern is to be joined as one, to consummate their marriage.

So too, when we pass from this world, we will be so occupied with our bridegroom that we will not be aware of the dinner party taking place by the mourners. Our attention will be with our bridegroom, who has taken us to His Father's house.

> *In My Father's house are many mansions; if it were not so, I would have told you. I go to prepare a place for you. And if I go and prepare a place for you, I will come again and receive you unto Myself; that where I am, there you may be also.* (John 14:2-3)

The word mansion in Aramaic is *ona,* which means a house with many rooms. In ancient times, a mansion was not built all at once. It would start as a single dwelling, and as children married, the sons would bring their wives to the family estate and build an addition to their father's house for themselves and their brides to live in. As more children grew, they would occupy their father's house—taking over rooms when the elders passed away or adding rooms if none were available.

Families lived together because it was the safest way to live in those days. There is safety in numbers, and you were more secure living with blood relatives. Eventually, these single dwellings became homes with many rooms, which we now call mansions. Today, using the word "mansion" in this verse can be misleading, as we often think of mansions as personally owned. Mansions in this context were family-owned and lived in by the family. Heaven is one big mansion with many rooms where we all live together with the Father.

This was the picture that Jesus was giving and what would have been understood by the disciples: that He, as the bridegroom, was going back to His Father's house to prepare a room for them to live with Him and become members of His family. Heaven is not dotted with rows and rows of houses but is one all-inclusive dwelling place for all the saints to live in harmony and love together for eternity.

So, if our marriage with God begins here on earth but is not consummated until we get to heaven, what is our relationship with Him like here on earth? It is a betrothal period, during which we are learning to grow in love with our bridegroom. We begin our journey to intimacy just as a bride and groom begin their journey into intimacy—with a hug.

Our experience with God will be in that *yichud* room with Him, where we will hug, and that hug will lead to a kiss, which will ultimately lead to an intimacy where we will truly become one with God.

It is fair to say that a betrothed couple was allowed to share hugs during their time of betrothal, as long as they were not lingering hugs that led to sexual arousal. They were exhorted to stop showing affection if they started to become physically aroused. There are different types of hugs: romantic hugs, passionate hugs, and friendly hugs. A hug is a form of endearment, found in virtually all human communities, in which two or more people put their arms around the neck, shoulder, back, or waist of one another and hold each other closely.

God created the hug to bring people closer together, to show someone you like them, or to share affection, acceptance, or value for that person.

Does it not stand to reason that God would then seek to give us hugs to show His affection for us and to show that He values us? What is a hug other than feeling close to someone and sensing their very presence? Is that not what we feel when we worship God?

A hug is the first step to intimacy. The next step would be a kiss. Before we receive the *Divine Kiss*, does it not follow that we will first receive a *Divine Hug*—perhaps many hugs from God before He actually kisses us? Does the Bible speak of a *Divine Hug*?

Hugging in the Bible is portrayed as a picture. The word that closely fits the concept of a hug is *chabaq*, which means "to draw close" and "to embrace." But there is another word that is even more intimate: *devequt*.

Genesis 2:24: *"Therefore shall a man leave his father and his mother, and shall cling unto his wife: and they shall be one flesh."*

Deuteronomy 4:4: *"But ye that did cling unto the LORD your God [are] alive every one of you this day."*

A man will still *chabaq* his mother and father—that is, he will embrace them—but with his wife, he will cling to her. This is not just a *chabaq*, an embrace, but something even more affectionate: it is a *devequt*.

When I hear the word *cling*, it gives me the impression of hanging on for dear life. You cling to a life jacket, or you cling to a rock on a ledge. The idea of a man clinging to his wife somehow does not create the picture I think God intended.

Practically every modern English translation uses a different word for *deveq* or *cling*. The NIV says *"united,"* the Living Bible says *"joined,"* the ESV says *"hold fast,"* the KJV says *"cleave,"* the CSB says *"bond,"* the CEV says *"married,"* and the ISV says *"cling."*

What is interesting is that the same word used for a man clinging to his wife is also used to describe how we are to relate to God. We are to cling to Him as a man clings to his wife.

How can we cling to God, and what does it mean to cling to your wife?

The problem lies in our understanding of the word *devequt*, which comes from the root word *deveq*. You see, we really cannot find a decent English

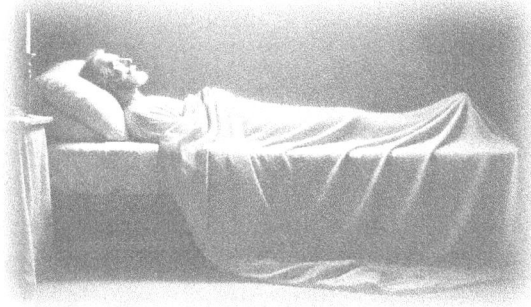

19. ABSENT OR PRESENT WITH THE LORD

"We are confident, I say, and willing rather to be absent from the body and to be present with the Lord." (II Corinthians 5:8)

I may have some Catholic friends who would take issue with the concept of the *Divine Kiss*, arguing that one must first spend some time in purgatory to burn off sins. Even the pope, according to Catholic teaching, must spend a little time in purgatory. Thus, they claim, you will not immediately experience that *Divine Kiss* or *Divine Hug* when your soul leaves your body.

Purgatory comes from the Latin word *purgatorium,* which refers to the belief in an intermediate state after death. It is understood as the final purification of the saint and is entirely different from the punishment of those in hell. Some traditions view this cleansing process as taking place in fire, though most imagine it as simply being in a state where one is not yet walking through the pearly gates, streets of gold, or mansions. It is a nonspecific place or condition of temporary suffering or torment.

The conception of purgatory as a physical place originated in Western Europe in 1274 at the Second Council of Lyon. The idea was that it would be a place of purifying fire, not punitive fire. More recently, Pope John Paul II and Pope Benedict XVI wrote that the term does not refer to a physical place but to a condition of existence.

The Church of England and most major Protestant and evangelical denominations reject the concept of purgatory. However, the Eastern Orthodox churches and some elements within the Anglican, Lutheran, and Methodist traditions hold that there may be a cleansing process after death. Most do not see it as a fiery purification or an actual place.

The Catholic Church derives its doctrine of an afterlife purification from II Maccabees 12:42-43. However, the book of Maccabees is regarded as apocryphal and not part of inspired Scripture or the canon in most Protestant and evangelical denominations. This passage provides the foundation for the Catholic belief that prayers and sacrifices for the dead can serve as a means to mitigate punishment for those who have passed.

For those in the Protestant faith, it is difficult to grasp the Catholic teaching that all who die in God's grace and friendship are still imperfectly purified and must undergo a process of purification. Popular imagination often sees purgatory as a physical place, but the Catholic doctrine does not actually describe it as such. Fire is also not a formal part of the doctrine. However, the paradox arises in the Church's teaching that the souls in purgatory benefit from the prayers and pious acts of the living. This seems to imply a time element, with different degrees of sin taking longer to purify than others. Yet, if purgatory exists outside time and space, the process should theoretically be instantaneous in the realm of God.

I discussed this issue with a friend of mine who was a retired Greek professor and Greek Orthodox priest. As a retired Hebrew teacher and a Baptist, I met with my Greek friend weekly for one-on-one Bible study. Our differing backgrounds and training led to some lively discussions. He used these sessions to brush up on his Hebrew while I brushed up on my Greek. However, when you put a Baptist and a Greek Orthodox priest together, there are bound to be some theological clashes. One area where we often "dueled" was on what happens to us the moment after we die—a topic that became more frequent as we aged.

He believed that we all go to a place where we await the final judgment. At that time, the saved would go to be with the Lord, and the unsaved would go to the lake of fire. While we expressed this differently, the ultimate conclusion was the same: we all end up where we are supposed to be. However, he admitted to a personal theory—unsupported by his church—that Jesus would be present in whatever place we go to immediately after death. He couldn't accept the idea of being separated from Jesus, even for a few hundred years or however long it might take to reach the final judgment.

As far as I'm concerned, we are on the same page. If I were to go to some holding place for purification and Jesus were right there with me, performing the purification rites, I wouldn't mind—even if it were purgatory. John 14:3 says, *"And if I go and prepare a place for you, I will come again and receive you unto myself, that where I am, there ye may be also."* Since I don't believe heaven is a literal place with mansions, streets of gold, or pearly gates, whatever place I end up in—if Jesus is there—that is heaven for me.

However, a third party entered our weekly studies and added confusion to our discussion. My friend had a close Roman Catholic friend who shared a profound personal experience. During surgery, his heart stopped beating, and he flatlined twice. Each time, he said he found himself instantly in heaven before Jesus, who told him it wasn't his time and sent him back. He described it as the most beautiful experience but said he could not put into words what he saw. Though he wanted to stay, Jesus sent him back.

I interrupted, asking, "Wait one minute! You mean to tell me you didn't go to purgatory? You went straight to heaven—no tunnel, no trip through space, nothing?"

"Nope," he replied. "I just stood before Jesus in heaven."

George, my Greek Orthodox friend, shook his head and said, "Well, I guess God can make exceptions."

Our Catholic friend couldn't explain it either. As a nominal Catholic who didn't attend Mass regularly, he had expected some time in purgatory. He thought he deserved it, so he was baffled by the experience. I suggested that perhaps Jesus was simply with him in purgatory, offering love and comfort during the purification process—like a father holding his child's hand during a root canal.

The real issue is that we cannot wrap our finite brains around the concept of living outside time and space. Personally, I believe that when Jesus died on the cross, He took all our sins upon Himself and suffered the punishment for them. There are no remaining sins for which we need purification. As far as I'm concerned, we can receive that *Divine Hug* and *Divine Kiss* from the very beginning.

Nonetheless, we had a great discussion about II Corinthians 5:8, *"We are confident, I say, and willing rather to be absent from the body and to be present with the Lord."* George read the verse to me in Greek, explaining that it doesn't necessarily mean we go straight to heaven. Paul uses the word *ekdemesai* (absent), which means "away from home" or "away from one's own type or nationality." The word for "to be present" is a similar term but with a *nu* rather than a *kappa,* meaning "to be among one's own kind or nationality."

I looked at this in the Aramaic text and found the word for "absent" is *na'nad,* from the root *'anad,* which is a nautical term for "going abroad" and is used euphemistically. When a sailor died at sea or did not return from a voyage, rather than saying he drowned or died at sea, they would simply say he "went abroad." Paul avoided calling the passing of a believer "death" because his concept of death was not the same tragic event most people envision. Instead, he used a euphemism, just as we do today. When someone dies, instead of using the harsh word "death," we say they "passed away" or "passed."

The Greek followed the same idea with a euphemism that essentially means a person "went away from home to be with their ancestors." This is very similar to the expression used in the Aramaic. However, the Aramaic word for "present"—as in "present with the Lord"—is *hua'*. This word is also used to describe a female and carries the connotation of being in the presence of someone filled with love, mercy, and nurturing. Idiomatically, it suggests the intimacy between a woman and a man, or, to avoid euphemism, a woman in a sexual relationship with a man.

The Greek, while less descriptive, conveys the idea that to be absent from the body is to be with one's own kind. The Aramaic, however, describes being absent from the body as sharing intimacy with God, much like a bride and bridegroom on their wedding day.

I believe this is why Paul uses the word *masuchinan,* from the root word *such,* when he says he is willing to be absent from the body and present with the Lord. The word "willing" (*masuchinan*) means "desire," but it is in the *Pael active participle* form, which intensifies the meaning from a simple desire to a deep longing. Paul is not merely desiring; he is longing—craving—to be absent from the body and present with the Lord.

Here, Paul is painting a picture of the consummation of a marriage between the bride and bridegroom. While on earth, we are only betrothed to Jesus; we cannot consummate our marriage to Him while in this corruptible, physical body. Once our soul leaves this sinful, fleshly body, it will join Jesus, consummating our relationship as His bride.

As a bridegroom anxiously waits and longs for the day they enter their *yichud* (bridal chamber) to consummate the marriage, Paul expresses the same longing to consummate his relationship with Jesus. The active participle form reflects not only Paul's longing but also the bridegroom's eagerness to seek and consummate the marriage.

Most of us are not as eager as Paul to leave this life and be joined with God, largely because of our fear of death. However, if we had experiences like Paul—his encounter with Jesus on the road to Damascus or being caught up into paradise—we might also be eagerly waiting and longing to leave this world behind.

For this reason, I am not inclined to believe there will be a separation from Jesus immediately after death to spend time in purgatory for purification. First, I believe Jesus has already done all the purification necessary. Second, I believe His *racham* love makes Him more eager to be joined with us than we are with Him. Why, then, would He not complete the purification process through His death on the cross?

If purgatory does exist, I agree with my Greek mentor: Jesus will be with us there, purifying us. And if that is the case, then purgatory itself would be heaven because of Jesus' presence.

If our Catholic friend is correct, then purgatory is instantaneous. In that case, I will rest on II Peter 3:8, *"But, beloved, be not ignorant of this one thing, that one day is with the Lord as a thousand years, and a thousand years as one day."*

If that one day is spent in purgatory, I am confident we will handle it just fine—especially if He continues giving us that *devekut* (*Divine Hug* and Kiss).

20. JOYFUL HOMECOMING

"Likewise, I say unto you, there is joy in the presence of the angels of God over one sinner that repenteth." (Luke 15:10)

Recently, my study partner and I walked up to her apartment, and I saw her two little Havanese dogs sitting at the window, anxiously waiting for her return. As soon as they saw her, the two little guys jumped down from the window and headed straight for the door. Sure enough, as she entered her apartment, she was greeted by her faithful little companions, delirious with joy and excitement over her return. They were jumping all over her, covering her in wet kisses and greeting her with joyful little yip-yip sounds.

I instantly thought of an old Aramaic word, *chadah,* which is used in Luke 15:10 for *"joy."* But the English word *joy* barely begins to tell the story of *chadah.*

Actually, *chadah* is a word used for a hot ember, like the glowing charcoal in your backyard grill. You pour lighter fluid over the coals, light them up, and let them heat. Then, when you blow on them, you see the hottest parts of the charcoal get even hotter and begin to glow a deep red. That glow you see from blowing on the embers is *chadah.*

The angels of God are already joyful, but when one sinner repents, their joy begins to "glow"—it becomes more intense. Note that this joy is in the presence of God. The Aramaic word for "presence" is *qadam,* which means "to stand in anticipation." When one sinner repents, the angels of God stand before Him, anticipating an outburst of joy—a greater glow of joy from the God they worship—over one sinner who comes home. Just as my study partner anticipates the outburst of joy from her little dogs, Moxie and Shiloh, when she comes home.

I recall driving my disability bus for an elderly woman who lived alone. I took her to the doctor every three weeks for a blood test. Every time I drove her home, I noticed a sense of *qadam* come over her as we approached her house. She anxiously awaited the moment we would pull up, and she would excitedly say: "There he is—my Maxwell, sitting by the window, waiting for me."

Maxwell was a big, beautiful German Shepherd who would jump all over this elderly woman as she walked through the door, covering her with wet kisses. It was as if she were Maxwell's whole world. She told me how Maxwell stood guard over her house, ready to protect her with his very life if necessary. She felt extremely safe around Maxwell, while everyone else—including myself—trembled in his presence. She also said Maxwell knew when she felt depressed. He would come to her, snuggle up, whimper, and try to cheer her up.

After helping her into the house and up the stairs to her porch, I would quickly return to my bus. I didn't want to confront Maxwell, but I would pause before driving off just to observe the warm greeting Maxwell gave his lonely companion. I always thought it was no coincidence that the word *dog* is *God* spelled backward.

Many years ago, a songwriter named Gilbert O'Sullivan wrote these lyrics in a number-one hit song:

It seems to me that
There are more hearts broken in the world
That can't be mended,
Left unattended.
What do we do?
What do we do?

Alone again, naturally.

It's amazing how such a melancholy song could become a number-one hit, but perhaps it resonated with so many because they related to the loneliness expressed by Gilbert O'Sullivan. My favorite artist is Vincent Van Gogh. One of his most famous paintings, *Irises,* depicts a cluster of blue-purple irises with one painted a bright white. That white iris stands alone in the painting, and most art historians agree that Van Gogh painted it to represent himself—lonely and isolated.

Loneliness is a real problem in modern society. Yet, if a lonely person would only repent, their eyes would open to the reality that their Creator and a heavenly host are waiting in *qadam*—anticipation—for them to turn to God. Even one seemingly insignificant individual can cause God to light up and glow with joy if they repent.

They say it's a tragedy when someone dies alone. Yet, a believer in God who has spent their life learning to love Him will never have to die alone. In fact, as believers, when we approach our eternal home, we will see God faithfully waiting by His window in heaven, watching for us—*qadam(ing),* anticipating our return with *chadah.*

I can't help but believe that God gave us gentle, loving creatures like Moxie and Shiloh, as well as fearsome yet loyal animals like Maxwell, to remind us that we never need to be lonely or fearful. There is a loving God sitting by the window of heaven, anxiously awaiting our arrival home so that He can *devekut*—hug us—and cover us with a big, warm *Divine Kiss.*

21. PAUL'S DIVINE KISS

And there came thither certain Jews from Antioch and Iconium, who persuaded the people, and, having stoned Paul, drew him out of the city, supposing he had been dead. (20) Howbeit, as the disciples stood round about him, he rose up, and came into the city: and the next day he departed with Barnabas to Derbe. (Acts 14:19-20)

I knew a man in Christ above fourteen years ago, (whether in the body, I cannot tell; or whether out of the body, I cannot tell: God knoweth;) such an one caught up to the third heaven. (3) And I knew such a man, (whether in the body, or out of the body, I cannot tell: God knoweth;) (4) How that he was caught up into paradise, and heard unspeakable words, which it is not lawful for a man to utter. (II Corinthians 12:2-4)

Some Bible scholars have suggested that Paul's visit to Paradise was a near-death experience (NDE), possibly triggered by his stoning at Lystra during his second missionary journey. We can only speculate whether this visit to Paradise was a near-death experience or simply a vision, as Scripture does not make it explicitly clear. However, there may be added clarity from the Aramaic.

Still, it seems from the wording in his second letter to the Corinthians that even the Apostle Paul was uncertain if he had a near-death experience when he said: *"Whether in the body, I cannot tell; or whether out of the body, I cannot tell: God knoweth."* This is intriguing—surely one would know if they had died. Yet, if one received a *Divine Kiss*, the transition from the natural to the supernatural world might not be as distinct as we tend to believe.

In a stoning, even a single stone is enough to kill or cause permanent damage. If anything, Paul was certainly knocked unconscious. However, that would not have been enough to stop an angry mob from continuing to throw stones. Everyone in the crowd would have taken their turn to ensure the victim's death.

Paul says he was *"caught up."* The Aramaic word for "caught up" is *chataph,* meaning to grab or take hold of quickly or instantly. This word appears in the *Ethpaal* form, which makes it a passive causative. Essentially, Paul was "caused to be snatched away." This form suggests that Paul had died from the stoning and was brought back to life. More than that, it implies that God snatched him away before the first stone even touched his body—he felt no pain at all.

In the Acts account, Paul's body was drawn out of the city, as they believed he was dead. The Aramaic word for "drawn out" is *garar,* meaning to roll, push, or drag, like moving a log. Most likely, they tied a rope around Paul to drag him out of town rather than carry him, as no one wanted to touch the bloody mess or get blood on their clothes.

They did not carry Paul's body because they believed he was dead. These were likely the same people who had stoned him. In a stoning, rocks are thrown or dropped on the head until it is reduced to a bloody pulp. Paul could not have survived such an ordeal. The verse says they "thought" he was dead. The Aramaic word *savar* means "to be confident." They were entirely sure he was dead.

It's curious why Paul would say in II Corinthians 12, *"And I knew such a man, (whether in the body, or out of the body, I cannot tell: God knoweth."* The Greek phrase *toiouton anthropin* means "such a man" or "like a man." Could it be that Paul is not referring to himself in this verse? In verse two, he says, *"a man in Christ"* (*anthropon en Christo* in Greek). This leaves room to wonder if Paul might be referencing Jesus in verse three rather than himself.

The Aramaic provides clarity, using the word *baranaish* in verse three, which literally means "the Son of a Woman"—an idiom for the Son of God, Jesus Christ. In verse two, Paul refers to himself as *nabara bamashiach,* meaning "a man in Christ." The Aramaic phrase *yadana,* translated as "I knew," comes from the root word *yada'* and implies intimacy—similar to the intimacy of the *Divine Kiss.* The syntax indicates that this knowing of *baranaish* (the Son of a Woman) occurred before Paul's visit to heaven.

Like Stephen, Paul was experiencing the *Divine Kiss* while being stoned.

With today's media—internet, television, radio, and publishing—we are inundated with testimonies and books from people claiming to have died and gone to heaven. Many of these accounts are questionable. Some are fabricated for attention or profit, while others are hallucinations or visions. Among these numerous testimonies, I believe a few are genuine.

My personal litmus test for evaluating these accounts is what they describe as the first thing they saw upon dying. Some mention seeing loved ones—parents, grandparents, or even pets. Others describe seeing an angel or a being they assume to be Jesus, leading them into a light. I dismiss these testimonies outright because if one truly saw Jesus, they would unmistakably know who He is.

Many give vivid descriptions of gates of pearl, streets of gold, and mansions but fail to mention the one essential element of heaven: Jesus Himself. At best, they describe hearing a voice telling them to return, without even clarifying if it was the voice of God or Jesus.

I've heard some testimonies in which Jesus supposedly gives the person a casual tour of heaven. One visiting speaker at a church I attended shared such an account, speaking about walls in heaven, gates of pearl, and even chariot races. The entire narrative felt absurd, as heaven does not require gates or walls to protect saints from external threats.

Biblically, I believe the first thing a true believer will see and experience is Jesus Christ Himself. Paul's account emphasizes intimacy with the Son of God: *"I knew such a man"* or, as rendered in the Aramaic, *"I was intimate with the Son of God."*

During Paul's experience, he "heard unspeakable words which were not lawful for a man to utter." The Greek phrase *arreta rhemata* refers to words or messages that are unspeakable or secret. These words may be unspeakable because they are either indescribable or forbidden to be revealed—perhaps both.

In Aramaic, the phrase "unspeakable words" is *mela dala matamalalan*. *Matamalalan* comes from the root word *mela*, which, in a *pael* (intensive) participle, means a complete message that is unexplainable. Thus, Paul would have liked to describe what he saw, but he could not—any more than someone from the first century could return from the 21st century and accurately explain airplanes, smartphones, television, the internet, automobiles, or other advanced technology.

For instance, Paul might try to explain an Apache helicopter firing a stinger missile as a "grasshopper with hair like a woman, a face like a man, and a sting that causes death." That would be a *mela dala matamalalan*—something unexplainable or indescribable because there is nothing in one's current understanding to accurately compare it to. Most likely, the gates of heaven and the walls of the heavenly city with streets of gold are not meant to be taken literally but are descriptions meant to convey something about the supernatural realm of God—something that cannot be fully explained until it is actually seen or experienced.

The Greek word for paradise is *paradesison,* which is derived from the Aramaic word *paradas*. This word literally means "garden" and is often used as a metaphor for a garden of esoteric knowledge. This is because Jewish tradition holds that the Garden of Eden is located in an alternate universe or another dimension existing alongside our natural dimension. It is their interpretation of heaven.

If heaven or the Garden of Eden is a place where there is no death, then there would be no plant life or animal life that dies. That would mean there is no consumption of plants or animals. How can something like that be explained unless it is understood esoterically or metaphorically? Thus, the concept becomes something very abstract, not easily explained in the natural realm.

For instance, you could not eat fruit from a tree, because once you remove the fruit from the tree, it loses its connection to the nourishment of life. When consumed, the fruit essentially "dies" to provide life to the one eating it. We have no concept of what the Garden of Eden was like except in terms of our natural, corrupt world, where death and the necessity of death are essential to the continuation of life.

Ultimately, there was only one thing Paul could explain, and even that was not fully adequate: the *Divine Kiss* that he received.

22. WHAT DID KING JEHOASH SEE

Then it came about, as they were going along and talking, that behold, there appeared a chariot of fire and horses of fire which separated the two of them. And Elijah went up by a whirlwind to heaven. And Elisha saw it and cried out, 'My father, my father, the chariots of Israel and its horsemen!' And he saw him no more. Then he took hold of his own clothes and tore them in two pieces. (II Kings 2:1)

Now Elisha was fallen sick of his sickness whereof he died. And Joash, the king of Israel, came down unto him, and wept over his face, and said, O my father, my father, the chariot of Israel, and the horsemen thereof. (II Kings 13:14)

Seventy years after the events of II Kings 2:11, we find a similar moment in II Kings 13:14, when Elisha lay dying in his bed. King Jehoash came to him, wept over him, and said: *"My father, my father, the chariots of Israel and its horsemen."* There is no doubt that for seventy years, Elisha told anyone who would listen about his experience with Elijah being taken to heaven in a chariot of fire. Then, as Elisha lay dying, you can only imagine how fitting it must have been for King Jehoash, his friend, to offer these same words of comfort—the very words Elisha had uttered seventy years earlier as he witnessed his mentor and best friend Elijah ascend to heaven.

King Jehoash was a godly king. His grandmother, Athaliah, was the daughter of Ahab and Jezebel and the wife of Jehoram, King of Judah. After the death of her son Ahaziah (Jehoash's father), Queen Athaliah usurped the throne and reigned for seven years. During her reign, she initiated a purge against the royal house of Judah, which included an attempt to kill her infant grandson, Jehoash. However, Jehoash's aunt, Jehosheba, who was married to the high priest Jehoiada, hid the infant in the Temple for seven years. Eventually, the high priest Jehoiada used his authority to crown and anoint Jehoash as king of Judah in a coup d'état against Athaliah, who was subsequently killed.

Under the guidance of his godly aunt and uncle, King Jehoash renewed the covenant between God, the king, and the nation. He destroyed the Tyrian worship of Baal that had been introduced under Jehoram and reinforced by Athaliah. The priest of Baal, Mattan, was executed, and the altars to Baal were demolished. For the first time in Judah's history, the Temple of Jerusalem and its priesthood achieved national prominence, with King Jehoash on the throne and Elisha serving as his chief advisor.

This background is significant because it shows that King Jehoash, despite his human flaws, led Judah into a massive spiritual revival and depended heavily on Elisha's prophetic guidance to govern the nation. Like Elisha, who witnessed the passing of Elijah, King Jehoash was allowed to see into the supernatural realm and witness what Elisha, lying on his deathbed, was also seeing.

In fact, I would take this one step further: God allowed Jehoash to experience the same divine moment that Elisha had experienced years earlier. When Elijah ascended, Elisha was caught up in a *tzimtzum*—a divine bubble, where he existed simultaneously in the physical and supernatural realms. Similarly, Jehoash may have been granted a glimpse into this "twilight zone," allowing him to see his friend and advisor pass into the arms of God and receive the *Divine Kiss*.

So, what did Jehoash see? Did he see a literal chariot and horsemen coming to take Elijah away?

I once found an artist's rendition of Elijah's ascension—a chariot pulled by two horses, fire blazing, with Elijah inside, waving goodbye to Elisha. But honestly, there is no way you could convince me that a literal wooden or even golden chariot, pulled by two flaming, flesh-and-blood horses, transported Elijah to heaven in the middle of a tornado. It's a thrilling Sunday School story, complete with a flannel graph depiction of Elijah in a fiery chariot. But after years of studying the Bible and biblical languages, I struggle to believe that Elijah needed a chariot with flying horses to reach heaven.

Either the "chariot of fire" is a metaphor, or alternative renderings from the Hebrew offer different insights.

First, Elijah was not taken to heaven in a chariot of fire but in a *s'ar*, which Rabbi Samson Hirsch describes as a swirling movement of energy. You might picture this as a whirlwind, but in modern terms, we might refer to it as a black hole or even a portal. If heaven exists outside this planet, a whirlwind—essentially air in motion—could not transport someone there, especially beyond the Earth's atmosphere. However, energy exists beyond our planet and possibly in other dimensions. Would it be any greater stretch of the imagination to envision this as a stargate, wormhole, or black hole rather than a literal whirlwind?

Physicists have theorized the existence of other realms, dimensions, or alternate universes that could potentially be accessed through black holes, wormholes, or portals. Is it really so far-fetched to imagine Elijah entering heaven through one of these phenomena rather than being transported in a chariot of fire?

Let's examine the Hebrew word for "chariot," *rakah. Rakah* refers to a means of transport powered by something other than oneself. In Modern Hebrew, *rakah* is used to describe a jet plane. If this account were written today, CNN would likely translate *rakah* from the Modern Hebrew as "jet aircraft" rather than "flying chariot." Essentially, Elijah passed into the next realm through a source of power not his own—a *rakah*.

Finally, consider the Hebrew word for "horses," *sus. Sus* is a common word in Semitic languages and denotes a connection between two points. The noun form of *sus* evolved to mean "horse" because horses were the primary mode of transportation between two points. In modern terms, we might think of *sus* as a "tunnel" or a connection. Passing through a portal or wormhole could be likened to passing through a tunnel connecting two realms—this world and the next.

The word *horseman* in Hebrew is *parash*. This is a very interesting word in its Semitic origins. In ancient times, it would translate as "horseman" or "charioteer," but in modern times, we might say "driver," "pilot," or "guide." That's exactly what a horseman or charioteer does—drive, pilot, or guide the horses. Within its Semitic root, the word *parash* literally means "to spread out your arms." A horseman riding a chariot would spread his arms, and thus the word evolved to mean a horseman or charioteer who is guiding, driving, or piloting his chariot.

Finally, the word *Israel* has various meanings and interpretations. It literally means "one who strives with God" or "struggles with God." According to many Jewish rabbis, this reflects the human struggle to achieve goodness and harmony with God. Another interpretation suggested by biblical scholars is "triumphant with God." Both meanings convey the idea of achieving victory, fulfilling one's purpose, and completing the mission God has for them after many struggles against the *yetzer hara*—the inclination toward evil, which drives one away from God.

Now let's revisit the phrase uttered by Elisha, and later by King Jehoash, as their closest friends and advisors departed this life: *"My father, my father, the chariots of Israel and its horsemen."*

The "chariots of Israel and its horsemen" could be a depiction of what Elisha saw when Elijah ascended into the realm of God—a vision of ultimate victory, the fulfillment of life's purpose and mission, and the moment of stepping into the outstretched arms of God. Under God's power and guidance, Elijah was taken to his eternal home. It was such a glorious moment that Elisha must have longed for the same experience himself and surely spoke of it often to his close friend, King Jehoash.

Years later, Jehoash was given the privilege of witnessing Elisha fulfill his lifelong dream of stepping into the arms of his Creator, once his earthly mission was complete, and being led to his eternal home.

This scene is more a picture of a *Divine Hug* than a *Divine Kiss*. First comes the hug, and then, as the portal closes, the *Divine Kiss*. For both Elijah and Elisha, these were not moments of tragedy or sorrow, but of joyous celebration. Those left behind may have felt the loss of a good friend and mentor, but they too likely experienced a sense of wistfulness and hope that one day, they might share in such an experience.

Personally, when my time comes, I don't want the first thing I see to be a former pet dog, my parents, or my grandparents. I have no interest in pearly gates, streets of gold, or mansions. I'm not even looking forward to having a mansion for myself. A small one-room cabin by a lake with a porch where Jesus and I can sit and talk would suit me just fine.

What I anticipate—and my one wish—is that when my time comes, there will be the chariots of Israel and its horsemen. In other words, I hope to see Jesus standing at the portal to heaven, arms spread wide, ready to give me that *Divine Hug*, followed by the *Divine Kiss*.

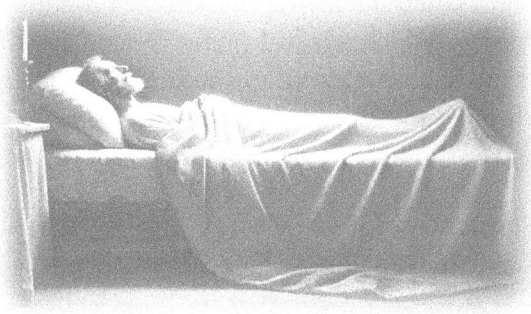

23. THE RAPTURE

"And they departed from the presence of the council, rejoicing that they were counted worthy to suffer shame for his name." (Acts 5:41)

> *For the Lord himself shall descend from heaven with a shout, with the voice of the archangel, and with the trump of God: and the dead in Christ shall rise first: Then we which are alive and remain shall be caught up together with them in the clouds, to meet the Lord in the air: and so shall we ever be with the Lord.* (I Thessalonians 5:16-17)

As I shared in the introduction to this book, I believe there is a very close relationship between the *Divine Kiss* and the rapture of the church. Both reflect a passing from this world to the next without fear, pain, or agony. In fact, the rapture is viewed as a time of great joy and celebration. So why is death considered so evil? Why don't we have the same longing for leaving this world through death as we do for leaving it through the rapture?

The only difference between the rapture and death for the believer is that, in the rapture, we will not die. However, at some point during the rapture, we would have to forfeit our physical bodies for something else. Our current physical bodies would not survive the transition, so we would need glorified bodies—like Jesus has, and like those resurrected will have.

For your consideration: Suppose I took my old, beat-up Nissan that's on its last set of tires into a shop and had it completely restored. When I get it back, it's like a completely new vehicle. Alternatively, for the same amount of money, I could purchase a brand-new Nissan with all the latest bells and whistles. Which would I prefer? Personally, I wouldn't care as long as it gets me to where I want to go. Similarly, whether I receive a glorified body through the rapture or through resurrection, what difference would it make as long as it takes me straight to the arms of Jesus?

But then you might say: "In the second case, you have to die, whereas in the rapture you don't." That takes us back to the original issue I raised in this book and in my introduction: Why do we fear death? Is it because we fear it will be painful?

Suppose you received a *Divine Hug* and *Kiss* before death so that you wouldn't even be conscious of any pain or suffering. A *Divine Hug* and Kiss would so preoccupy your consciousness that you wouldn't even be aware of your soul leaving your body. It would be like being put under anesthesia before major surgery. Without the anesthesia, you would endure unbearable pain as the surgeon cuts into your body. But thanks to modern medical science, you can go through surgery without any pain.

Before surgery, you may feel anxiety over potential complications or disabilities. But imagine if Jesus came to your bedside, took your hand, and said, *"Time to join me in eternity."* The delight of seeing His face, feeling His presence, experiencing His overwhelming *racham* love, and sensing His gentle touch would replace all your fears. You wouldn't feel any anxiety over disability or death. In fact, you would feel pure anticipation—no longer hindered by any earthly concerns.

All you would think, feel, and long for is to be joined as one with the God who loves you and the God you love in return.

Then there is the fear of separation from friends and family in death, whereas in the rapture, all your friends and family will be with you. I can understand that hesitation, but in death, you will be joining many more friends and family members who have already gone on before you. Additionally, we all have friends and family members who have not yet given their lives to Jesus and would be left behind. So, you would still experience separation either way.

In fact, there would be little hope that those left behind would be saved in the rapture, whereas in death there will still be plenty of believers to help ensure your loved ones join you when it's their time. Also, remember that you are entering a realm where time does not exist. The separation would feel like only a moment, like a fleeting separation in a dream where you awaken to find all your loved ones present with you.

So, why do we so fear death, to the point that we dream, hope, and pray for the rapture to occur? To me, the rapture and death sound pretty much the same. In fact, death becomes a little more desirable than the rapture. At least your unsaved loved ones would still have a chance to find peace with God.

Hanging high in the sky without a parachute seems far more terrifying than being whisked away into the loving arms of Jesus and into Paradise. I can already hear you saying, *"But isn't that what the rapture is—being whisked away into the loving arms of Jesus?"*

That's my point exactly—they are the same thing.

The verses above from I Thessalonians are the hallmark verses for the rapture of the church.

If we take a literal interpretation of these verses, we see a clear teaching about an unprecedented event in human history. A massive number of people will be taken up by Jesus when He returns to bring all those who have been born again to heaven with Him. First, all those who have died will be resurrected from their graves in glorified bodies and taken to heaven, leaving behind those who remain to face seven years of tribulation.

I grew up traumatized by the fear that the rapture would occur, and I'd be left behind. That's why I now prefer to just ignore the debate about whether the rapture is an actual event or simply a metaphor. If such an event does happen in my lifetime, that's fine and dandy. However, at my age, the odds of it happening while I'm still alive shrink with each passing day.

So, I'm not going to mount any defense for or against the teaching of the rapture because, to me, it no longer matters. Whether I'm taken to heaven in the rapture or through the *Divine Kiss*, it's all the same.

As I described in my introduction, if given the choice at the time of the rapture to either be taken to the marriage supper of the Lamb or to remain on this earth for seven more years to experience the Great Tribulation—where I'd likely end up as a martyr through some horrible and painful death—I'd choose staying behind, hands down.

What? Am I some sort of masochist?

Well, I read in Acts 5:41: *"And they departed from the presence of the council, rejoicing that they were counted worthy to suffer shame for his name."*

If martyrdom were to occur, I am persuaded and convinced that I would receive a *Divine Hug* and *Divine Kiss*. To me, volunteering for tribulation duty and forgoing the rapture is a win-win.

The Aramaic word for "suffering shame" is *tsatar*, which literally means "to inflict pain." In its *Ethpael* form, this word becomes intensive, meaning more than just shame—it signifies torture. The apostles rejoiced that they were considered worthy to endure *tsatar* (torture) for the sake of Jesus' name. I have read many stories of Christians who were tortured for their faith, and though they suffered pain, they also testified to experiencing something others did not: the healing presence of God.

Now, let's focus on the rapture. There's one aspect of the rapture teaching that has always bothered me. Imagine a 21st-century Christian in the United States—someone who has never faced real persecution, who has enjoyed the benefits of faith, such as healing and prosperity—being raptured before even feeling the slightest heat of suffering. Yet, many faithful believers throughout history have endured lifetimes of suffering and persecution for their faith, ending in death.

Why wouldn't these faithful believers also be given the benefit of a rapture, leaving the world without dying? I struggle to believe in a God who would be so unfair.

It is for this reason that I have written this book on the *Divine Kiss* and *Divine Hug*.

I believe in a fair and just God. Therefore, I cannot believe the rapture is reserved for "spoiled Christians" afraid of getting their toes burned. God is the rewarder of faithfulness, and His reward is not a mansion in heaven, toll-free access to walk streets of gold, or pearly gates. His reward is the flood of His infinite love, tenderness, gentleness, and peace—what I call *racham* love.

This love is reserved equally for every one of His faithful followers. His reward is deliverance from this world without the fear, terror, or agony of death. Even though the physical body may die, His presence will so overwhelm, encompass, and surround the faithful believer that the sufferings of this world and of the body will fade. The transition from this world to the next will be indistinguishable from the rapture itself.

I offer you a new definition of the rapture of the church. It is not limited to those alive when the Lord returns but extends to all who have been faithful to the end. I call it the *Secret Rapture,* also known as the *Divine Kiss* of the church. If you happen to be in the midst of persecution, the *Divine Kiss* will make you eligible for the *Divine Hug.* In fact, God will give you a *Divine Hug* even if you are not persecuted—as long as you have sought harmony with Him.

24. ALL CREATION TEACHES A DIVINE KISS

But ask now the beasts, and they shall teach thee; and the fowls of the air, and they shall tell thee: Or speak to the earth, and it shall teach thee: and the fishes of the sea shall declare unto thee. Who knoweth not in all these that the hand of the LORD hath wrought this? In whose hand is the soul of every living thing, and the breath of all mankind. (Job 12:7-10)

"If there are no dogs in Heaven, then when I die I want to go where they went."—Will Rogers

It is really interesting that the word *teach* in Hebrew in this passage is not the usual word for "teach," which is *lamed.* There are occasions when the word *laqach* is rendered as "teach," but rarely do we find that the word used in Job 12:7-8 is rendered as "teach." It is the word *toreka,* which comes from the root word *yarad.*

This is the same word found in Genesis 1:28:

And God blessed them, and God said unto them, Be fruitful, and multiply, and replenish the earth, and subdue it: and have dominion over the fish of the sea, and over the fowl of the air, and over every living thing that moveth upon the earth.

As I look at all the modern Christian translations of the Bible, I find that without exception, every one of them follows the common teaching that the word *yiredu* comes from the root word *radah,* which means to have dominion, to dominate, or to subdue. It is also a word used to express the idea of ruling over or treading upon, as in a winepress. Yet, many years ago, an old orthodox rabbi taught me that the root word was not *radah* but *yarad,* which means to lower yourself or to come down to the level of another.

This word carries the idea of showing respect and honor. It is the picture of a king stepping down from his throne to sit with one of his subjects and have a friendly conversation about personal matters. Since then, I have read numerous stories of rabbis and sages who were able to communicate with animals through *yiredu*—bringing themselves down from their lofty position to honor and respect God's creation and then listening to the messages of these lowly creatures.

Many years ago, I was walking through a shopping mall where the Future Farmers of America had set up some displays. One display was a 10-foot-by-10-foot area enclosed by a 4-foot-high fence. The floor of the display area was covered with hay, and in the center of the pen were two little lambs. Naturally, there was a crowd around the fence, with children calling out to the lambs and throwing hay at them, trying to get their attention. But the lambs just ignored everyone.

As I approached the fence, I recalled how certain rabbis worshiped God with their animals. So, I placed my hands on the railings and began to quietly worship and praise God alongside the two lambs, who I believed were also in a state of worship to God.

Suddenly, the two lambs looked up in my direction. The crowd hushed as the lambs moved away from the center of the pen and slowly walked toward me. They came up to me and pressed their noses against the knuckles of my hand, which was resting on the fence rail. The people around me began asking questions, assuming I was the owner of the lambs. I thought about explaining *yiredu* to them but decided against it, figuring, *"What's the use?"*

God intended for His creation to be one large classroom for us. His animals, birds, and fishes are our teachers, meant to teach us about His nature, communicate messages of love and care, and reveal the reality of sin.

Once, while teaching a Hebrew class to a group of inner-city pastors, I discussed *yiredu,* or communicating with God's creation. I noticed their doubtful expressions, so I decided to demonstrate. We were in the basement of an inner-city church, located in what's often called a "concrete jungle." The only wildlife around were the street gangs.

I walked around the block one day before class and realized there were no trees. Children growing up in this area might never see a tree. Without trees, there were no birds. So, in class, I used a method I had learned from rabbinical teaching and called a little bird to join us. Suddenly, a bird appeared and perched on the blackboard, right above the word *yiredu,* which I had written. The bird bobbed its head, then flew off. The pastor of the church, amazed, said there had never been a bird in their basement before. The other pastors' doubtful looks disappeared.

In *Journey into Silence* I discuss communicating with animals in more detail. But to keep this brief, let me just say: The next time a dog stops and stares at you, or a squirrel runs up and twitches its nose at you, stop and consider—maybe God is trying to tell you something through *yiredu.*

The Talmud teaches that when a little bird lands near you and starts to sing and dance, it's reminding you that the Holy Spirit is near your heart. Stop and listen. Ask yourself what the Holy Spirit might be trying to say.

Job 12:7 tells us, *"The fowls of the air will tell us."* The word *tell* in Hebrew is *yagad,* from the root word *nagad,* which means "to demonstrate," "to sensitize," or "to cause you to respond to certain stimuli." So, if a bird lands near you and starts singing, pay attention. It might be trying to tell you that the Spirit of God is near and has a message for you.

One day, while driving a woman home from a doctor's appointment in my disability bus, I learned she had received some disturbing news. I decided to use a little *yiredu* and called a bird to meet her at her house. Sure enough, when we arrived, there was a little bird on her porch, singing and dancing.

I pointed it out to her, saying, "Oh look, a little bird is here to greet you!" She grunted, "He's just going to poop on my porch," and waved her hand, saying, "Scat." I swear that little bird looked heartbroken as it flew away—or perhaps I just imagined it.

The word *angel* in Hebrew is *malech,* which simply means "messenger." Have you ever seen an angel or messenger of God? Look out your window—there might be a *malech* in your backyard, singing and dancing to deliver a message of love from God. Perhaps a little squirrel pauses in its busy life to twitch its nose at you, as if to say, "Hey, God provided these nuts for me; how much more will He provide for you?"

Years ago, when I was a pastor, I woke up one morning feeling deeply depressed. The pressures of church problems were overwhelming me. I decided to visit one of my favorite congregants, Esther, who was always joyful and filled with the presence of God. I knew a little time with her would lift my spirits.

When I arrived at her door, I was greeted with the expected joyful greeting from Esther, who enthusiastically invited me into her home. She joyfully declared: "Oh, I am so glad you came by. Come, come, I just have to tell you the message the Lord gave me." As we sat down at her kitchen table, she told me how she woke up that morning feeling so lonely and depressed. Her husband of sixty years had recently passed, and she was really missing him that particular morning.

As she sat at her kitchen table, feeling sorry for herself, a little bird began tapping on her window. She was annoyed and chased the bird away. But he returned and continued tapping at her window. This time, as she jumped up to chase the bird away, the bird flew off before she reached the window, landing on the lawn in her backyard. He did a little dance, then flew up to a tree, sang a song, and returned to her window. By this time, Esther knew the little fellow was delivering a message from God.

She had a revelation of the joy of the Lord, and the Lord spoke to her heart, saying: "The joy that my little feathered creation is bringing to you is only a small taste of the joy you bring to me as you continue your journey on the earth, bringing joy to those who need encouragement." Then, of course, just a few minutes later, her discouraged and frustrated pastor came to her door, seeking words of encouragement in the Lord.

As I felt uplifted by Esther's encouraging words, I realized that this little circle of joy—from the bird to Esther to me—completed its circle in bringing joy to the Heavenly Father.

I wonder if, when I pass from this world and am greeted with the *Divine Kiss* of God, I will see a little bird singing and dancing on God's shoulder, reminding me of the joy I brought to Him when I allowed His little bit of creation to bring me joy.

As I grow older in my walk with God, I find myself growing closer and closer to His heart. The closer I draw to God's heart, the more aware I am of His creation and the more appreciative I am of it. I am beginning to see the love of God all around me.

I remember, as a small child, being with my grandmother in a park during the fall season, when the leaves were changing colors and falling from the trees. I asked my grandmother why the leaves turned such beautiful colors. She told me that God created every green leaf for a purpose. Its mission on this earth was to provide life-giving oxygen.

Then, when it came time for the little green life to die—as all life on earth must, once it fulfills its earthly mission—God gives each leaf a kiss, and that little green leaf gives us one last gift: it turns into something beautiful. Then, waving her hand over the majestic scene of a forest filled with the glorious colors of fallen leaves, she said: "Never forget that when it comes time for us to die, God will give us a kiss and make us into something beautiful."

The Jewish sages call it a *Divine Kiss*.

Because if you would confess with your mouth the Lord Y'shua and you would believe in your heart that God raised Him from the dead, you will be saved: for he believes for himself in his heart into righteousness, and confesses for himself with his mouth into salvation. (Romans 10:9-10 *One New Man Bible*)

ABOUT THE AUTHOR

Chaim Bentorah is a former Hebrew Instructor at World Harvest Bible College, where he taught Hebrew, Old Testament, and Church History for seventeen years. He is a graduate of Moody Bible Institute with a B.A. in Jewish Studies and earned his M.A. in Hebrew and Old Testament from Denver Seminary. He also earned his Ph.D. in Biblical Archaeology.

During his time in graduate school, he studied under Dr. Kalland, who served on the executive committee for the translation of the New International Version of the Bible. Chaim and another student earned graduate credit working with Dr. Kalland on his translations. After experiencing the inner workings involved in a major translation, he sought out Jewish rabbis, discovering a broader and deeper perspective on translating the Old Testament from the Hebrew.

He has brought this understanding into over fifteen books on Hebrew and Aramaic word studies, introducing the wisdom of Jewish teachers spanning over 3,000 years through the Talmud, Midrash, Targum, and other Jewish literature.

Chaim Bentorah's blog includes over 2,500 word studies from Hebrew, Greek, and Aramaic.

Chaim and his study partner, Laura Bertone, host a paid online learning platform at www.hebrewwordstudy.com where they teach two live classes a week and offer courses in learning how to use Hebrew and Aramaic in personal study of the Old and New Testaments.

To learn more about Chaim Bentorah's books and word studies please visit www.chaimbentorah.com.

OTHER BOOKS BY CHAIM BENTORAH

- A Hebrew Teacher Explores Psalm 23: Discovering Life's Journey
- Palal: A Hebrew Teacher Explores Prayer
- Aramaic Word Study II: Discover God's Heart In The Language Of The New Testament
- Swimming In His Presence: A Hebrew Teacher Reflects On Worship and Praise
- Aramaic Word Study: Exploring The Language Of The New Testament
- Stargates, Time Travel, And Alternate Universes
- Time Loop: Seeing America's Future in Persia's Past
- Hebrew Word Study: Exploring The Mind Of God
- Ten Words That Will Change Everything You Know About God
- Does The Bible Really Sat That?
- Treasures of the Deep
- Learning God's Love Language
- Learning God's Love Language Workbook
- Hebrew Word Study: Revealing The Heart Of God
- Journey into Silence
- Whom My Soul Loves
- Intimacy With God
- Is This Really Revival?
- Biblical Truths From Uncle Otto's Farm